KB181953

Smart Vocabulary

3

집필진: 김미희, E·NEXT 영어연구회
김미희, 박경희, 박소현, 임지연, 홍정민, 한성욱, Christina KyungJin Ham, Leeanne Madden(Editorial Advisor)

김미희 선생님은 이화여자대학교 영어교육과를 졸업하고 EBS English에서 방영하는 'Yo! Yo! Play Time'과 'EBS 방과
우 영어'를 십씰 및 검토하셨으며, 베스트셀러인 '10시간 영문법'과 '영어 글쓰기왕 비법 따라잡기' 등의 많은 영어교재
를 집필하셨습니다. E·NEXT 영어연구회는 김미희 선생님을 중심으로, 세계 영어교육의 흐름에 발맞추어 효과적이고
바람직한 영어 교수·학습 방법을 연구하는 영어교육 전문가들의 모임입니다.

Smart Vocabulary 3

지은이 김미희
펴낸이 정규도
펴낸곳 다락원

초판 1쇄 발행 2011년 10월 10일
초판 8쇄 발행 2022년 11월 10일

편집장 최주연
책임편집 장경희, 오승현
영문교정 Michael A. Putlack
아트디렉터 정현석
디자인 윤미주, 김은미, 이승현

다락원 경기도 파주시 문발로 211
전화: (02)736-2031 내선 251~252
Fax: (02)732-2037
출판등록 1977년 9월 16일 제406-2008-000007호

Copyright ⓒ 2011 김미희

저자 및 출판사의 허락 없이 이 책의 일부 또는 전부를 무단
복제·전재·발췌할 수 없습니다. 구입 후 철회는 회사 내규
에 부합하는 경우에 가능하므로 구입문의처에 문의하시기
바랍니다. 분실·파손 등에 따른 소비자 피해에 대해서는 공
정거래위원회에서 고시한 소비자 분쟁 해결 기준에 따라 보
상 가능합니다. 잘못된 책은 바꿔 드립니다.

값 9,500원

ISBN   978-89-277-4027-8
        978-89-277-4030-8(set)

http://www.darakwon.co.kr
다락원 홈페이지를 통해 책 속의 영문 해석 자료,
표제어 및 스토리 MP3 파일을 받아 보실 수 있습니다.

출간에 도움 주신 분들

신가윤(Brown International School 국제학교 분당캠퍼스 원장)
배정연(키디리교육센터 메인 강사)
Jeniffer Kim(English Hunters 원장)
전남숙(KidsCollege 원장)
Leigh Stella Lage(성남외국어고등학교 원어민교사)
조은정(아이스펀지 잉글리쉬 원감)
심희선 이영란 박종희
이선옥(OK's Class 원장)

내지일러스트 강선용   표지일러스트 노유이

Smart Vocabulary를 추천합니다!

단어 공부는 외국어 공부의 기본이자 실력입니다. 단어 공부에 대한 의견이 분분하지만, 영어를 제 2외국어로 삼고 있는 우리 어린이들에게 단어 학습이 필요하다는 사실은 부정할 수 없습니다. 문제는 방법이지요. 단어의 철자와 뜻만 외우는 것은 너무 단편적이어서 큰 의미가 없습니다. 어린이들이 쉽고 재미있게 단어를 익히면서 실생활에서 활용할 수 있는 효과적인 단어 학습 방법이 필요합니다. 그런 의미에서, 기계적인 암기에서 끝나지 않고 꼭 필요한 단어들을 이야기 속에서 익힐 수 있는 **WOW! Smart Vocabulary** 시리즈를 적극 추천합니다.

김정렬 (한국교원대학교 영어교육과 교수, 초등영어교과서 저자, 한국초등영어교육학회 회장)

제시된 단어를 문제 풀이를 통해 이해 수준을 확인하던 기존의 어휘 학습 방법을 탈피하여, 학습자가 관심을 가질 수 있는 다양한 주제의 어휘들을 논픽션과 픽션으로 이루어진 스토리와 연계해서 자연스럽게 학습할 수 있는 점이 **WOW! Smart Vocabulary** 시리즈의 가장 큰 특징이라고 할 수 있습니다. 또한 워크북은 배운 단어들을 스스로 정리하고 확실히 익히는 데 매우 효과적인 문제 유형들로 이루어져 있네요.

샤이니 김재영 (EBS English 영어방송진행자)

단어를 많이 아는 것도 중요하지만 실제 생활에서 상황에 맞는 단어를 활용하는 것이 더욱 중요합니다. 같은 단어라 할지라도 때론 문장 속에서 여러 의미로 해석되기도 하고, 다른 뜻으로 쓰여지기도 합니다. **WOW! Smart Vocabulary** 시리즈는 초등학교에서 중학교까지 단계적으로 단어를 학습할 수 있도록 구성되어 있으며, 스토리 속에서 살아 움직이는 단어를 익혀 실제 생활에 활용할 수 있도록 전략적으로 구성되어 있어 재미와 지식, 단어의 실제적 활용을 동시에 잡는 단어 교재라고 여겨집니다.

조은옥 (성지초등학교 교감, 초등영어교과서 저자)

한 주제별로 논픽션, 픽션의 두 가지 레슨이 짝으로 이루어진 점이 아주 신선하네요. 또한 스토리 속에 학습 단어들을 적용해 가며나의 단어帳 만들어 갈 수 있게 해주는 구성도 마음에 듭니다. Unit마다 쉬운 단어부터 난이도 있는 단어 학습까지 할 수 있어서 학습자가 성취감을 느낌과 동시에 난이도 있는 단어에도 도전 정신을 갖도록 해주는 것이 이 책의 큰 매력입니다.

이수진 (코너스톤 국제학교 아카데믹매니저)

WOW! Smart Vocabulary 시리즈는 초등학교뿐 아니라 중학교 수준의 필수 어휘까지 주제에 맞게 학습할 수 있습니다. 단순히 뜻을 외우거나 어휘의 기능에만 초점을 두는 학습이 아니라 어휘의 문법적인 쓰임과 실용적인 표현을 통한 문장 활용까지 배울 수 있게 구성한 것이 좋습니다. 더 나아가 스토리 속에서 어휘를 익힘으로써 어휘 교재이면서도 어휘 수준을 능가하는 의미 있는 학습을 제공한다는 점이 큰 장점이라고 할 수 있습니다. 또한 효율적인 연습 문제 유형들도 돋보입니다.

박진희 (중탑초등학교 교사)

WOW! Smart Vocabulary has various nonfiction and fiction stories which give this book its charm. These interesting stories will keep students motivated. Along with engaging exercises, students are sure to efficiently learn new words from this book.

Janet Y Ko (용마초등학교 원어민 교사)

이 책의 구성과 특징

WOW! Smart Vocabulary에는 여러 영어 교육 전문가 선생님들이 오랜 시간 동안 현장에서 직접 적용해보고 지도해본 실제 경험이 고스란히 녹아 들어가 있습니다.

모든 Unit은 하나의 주제 아래 Nonfiction과 Fiction이라는 두 개의 쌍둥이 Lesson으로 이루어져 있습니다.

첫 번째 Lesson에서는 실화, 신문기사, 광고 등과 같이 사실적인 정보를 주는 이야기(Nonfiction)를 통해 단어들을 익힙니다.

두 번째 Lesson에서는 주인공과 함께 친구가 되어 가상의 이야기(Fiction) 속에 빠져들면서 단어를 배우게 됩니다.

표제어 + 빈칸에 써 보기

주제에 따라 서로 연관성이 있는 표제어들을 제시하기 때문에 기억하기 쉽습니다. 사진이나 삽화를 통해 각 단어의 분명한 의미를 바로 파악할 수 있고, 빈칸에 직접 단어를 써 보면서 단어를 눈에 익히게 함으로써 시각적 연상을 통해 단어를 감각적으로 기억할 수 있습니다.

※ 단어 선정과 분류는 교육부 개정교육과정 기본어휘 목록표를 바탕으로 했으며, 이 외에도 실제 초등학생의 일상생활에서 친숙한 단어와 중학 영어 학습을 위해 꼭 알아두어야 할 단어까지 함께 제시했습니다.

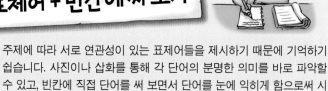

단계적인 연습문제

단계적인 연습문제 풀이를 통해 단어에서 구로, 구에서 문장으로 점진적으로 나아갑니다.
학습하는 단어와 관련하여 기억하기 쉽게 도와주는 확장형 연상문제도 있습니다.
단어의 철자만 익히는 것이 아니라, 그 단어가 문장 속에서 어떻게 쓰이는지 학습할 수 있습니다.

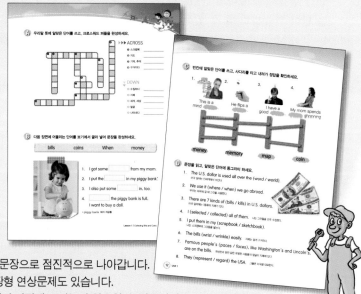

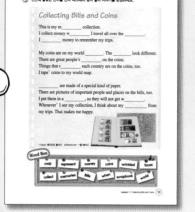

스토리 구성하기

각 Lesson의 마지막 단계는 Lesson에서 제시하는 학습단어들로 스토리를 만드는 것입니다. 논픽션과 픽션의 재미있는 쌍둥이 스토리 속에 녹아 있는 학습단어를 찾아 쓰면서, 배운 단어들이 실제 스토리 속에서 어떻게 살아 움직이는지 경험해 봅니다.

별책부록 - 워크북

본책의 각 Unit에서 배운 학습단어의 우리말 뜻을 보고 단어를 써 보며 스스로 실력을 체크하고, 각 Lesson마다 등장하는 스토리 속 문장을 통해 다시 한번 학습단어를 점검합니다.
이어지는 Review Test에서는 단어의 단순 암기가 아닌 실용적인 활용에 중점을 두고 구성한 다양한 유형의 문제들을 풀어보면서 실력을 확인해 봅니다.

학습 예시

WOW! Smart Vocabulary는 총 5권으로 구성되어 있고, 권 당 10개의 Unit, 한 Unit에 두 개의 Lesson이 들어있습니다.
한 Lesson을 학습하는 데 약 한 시간이 걸리므로,
한 Unit을 대체로 두 시간 동안 학습할 수 있습니다.
WOW! Smart Vocabulary를 일주일에 5시간 학습할 경우 권 당 4주, 총 5개월 정도가 소요됩니다.

	학습 시간	Unit / Lesson	표제어 수 & 비율	Total
1권	20시간 Lesson 당 1시간	10/20	Unit별 20개(Lesson별 10개) 교육부 제시 초등 기본어휘 70~80% / 중등 기본어휘 + 확장어휘 20~30%	200
2권	20시간 Lesson 당 1시간	10/20	Unit별 20개(Lesson별 10개) 교육부 제시 초등 기본어휘 60~70% / 중등 기본어휘 + 확장어휘 30~40%	200
3권	20시간 Lesson 당 1시간	10/20	Unit별 24개(Lesson별 12개) 교육부 제시 초등 기본어휘 50~60% / 중등 기본어휘 + 확장어휘 40~50%	240
4권	20시간 Lesson 당 1시간	10/20	Unit별 24개(Lesson별 12개) 교육부 제시 초등 기본어휘 40~50% / 중등 기본어휘 + 확장어휘 50~60%	240
5권	20시간 Lesson 당 1시간	10/20	Unit별 28개(Lesson별 14개) 교육부 제시 초등 기본어휘 30~40% / 중등 기본어휘 + 확장어휘 60~70%	280
총 학습단어 수				1,160

3권 단어구성표

3권		초등 기본어휘	중등 기본어휘	확장 어휘	표제어 수
Unit 1 **My** **Collection**	Lesson 1 Collecting Bills and Coins	map, face, when, money, world	bill, coin, memory, collect, represent	wrinkle, scrapbook	24
	Lesson 2 Lucy's Nap with Her Dolls	with, light, where, always, cloudy	alive, prize, proud, stage, contest	hug, nap	
Unit 2 **Amazing** **B-Boy** **Dancers**	Lesson 1 Korean B-Boy Teams	hard, dance, every, great, another, pleased, give a big hand	spin, speed, amazing, support	teenager	24
	Lesson 2 A B-Boy Prince	pull, role, swim, prince, street, handsome, together, go down on one's knees	appear, partner, perform	fantastic	
Unit 3 **Murphy's** **Law**	Lesson 1 The Meaning of Murphy's Law	call, hour, pass, example, problem, school bag	law, scold, decide, annoyed	Coke, wallet	24
	Lesson 2 An Unlucky Day	miss, hurry, wrong, office, unlucky, fall on one's face	reach, barely, balance, mechanic, suddenly	wedding	
Unit 4 **Mom's** **Words**	Lesson 1 To My Lovely Daughter	hope, word, knock, future, honest, come true	healthy, regularly, various, postpone, challenge, important		24
	Lesson 2 Mom's Nagging	read, wait, wash, brush, homework, make a bed	comb, share, exercise	chew, nagging, oversleep	
Unit 5 **Bookworm**	Lesson 1 Children's Book Awards	get, best, some, check, right, choose	vote, award	fiction, bookmark, bookworm, book report	24
	Lesson 2 A Gift from Harry	fan, dark, hold, spell, voice, ask for, become, mirror	rush, brave	dragon, wizard	

3권		초등 기본어휘	중등 기본어휘	확장 어휘	표제어 수
Unit 6 **About Cars**	Lesson 1 Ford Model T	low, rich, cheap, first, price, middle class	mass, effect, system, quality, produce	slogan	24
	Lesson 2 A Flying Car	far, road, really, at last, get in[on], airplane, traffic jam	stick, shake, severe, happen	dizzy	
Unit 7 **At the Beach**	Lesson 1 Boracay Beach	fat, sell, beach, relax, visitor, water fight	lie, view, along, shallow, sandcastle	surf	24
	Lesson 2 Hi, Mr. Dolphin	sea, deep, get to, laugh, inside, vacation	dive, spit, breath, swallow, slippery	glittering	
Unit 8 **I Enjoy Cooking**	Lesson 1 How to Make Chicken Curry	carrot, potato, minute, chicken, how to+동사원형, health	fry, add, oil	peel, onion, ingredient	24
	Lesson 2 Giggle Gaggle Cooking Contest	egg, hen, well, happy, tooth, enough	mix, pot, chef, topic	simmer, fridge	
Unit 9 **At the Hospital**	Lesson 1 In the Emergency Room	hurt, stay, worry, hospital	treat, crowded, patient, headache	emergency, bleed, bandage, symptom	24
	Lesson 2 Lucy Becomes a Doctor	ill, be able to, excellent, take a rest, fall in love, stomachache	pretend, instead of	clinic, disguise, give a shot, prescribe	
Unit 10 **Roller Coaster**	Lesson 1 Why Do People Like Roller Coasters?	top, guess, rider, which, because	fear, while, located, increase, rapidly	thrill, at the same time	24
	Lesson 2 An Adventure with a Genie	buy, gate, seat, thirsty, yesterday	lamp, steal, escape, moment, imagine, adventure	maze	

Contents

Wow! Smart Vocabulary

3

Unit 1
My Collection

✪ 초등 기본어휘 　◯ 중등 기본어휘 　⬤ 확장어휘

1

✪ **map**
　명 지도

map

2

✪ **face**
　명 얼굴

face

3

✪ **when**
　접 ~할 때
　부 언제

when

4

✪ **money**
　명 돈

money

5
✪ **world**
　명 세계, 세상
　유 universe 우주, 세계

world

6

◯ **bill**
　명 지폐

bill

7

◯ **coin**
　명 동전

coin

8

◯ **memory**
　명 기억, 추억
　동 memorize 기억하다

memory

9

◯ **collect**
　동 수집하다, 모으다
　명 collection 수집품

collect

10

◯ **represent**
　동 나타내다, 상징하다
　유 stand for ~을 상징하다

represent

11

⬤ **wrinkle**
　동 구겨지다, 주름이 지다

wrinkle

12

⬤ **scrapbook**
　명 스크랩북

scrapbook

A 우리말 뜻에 알맞은 단어를 쓰고, 크로스워드 퍼즐을 완성하세요.

▶▶▶ ACROSS

❶ 스크랩북 _____

❺ 지도 _____

❼ 기억, 추억 _____

❾ 구겨지다 _____

▼ DOWN

❷ 수집하다 _____

❸ 지폐 _____

❹ 세계, 세상 _____

❻ 얼굴 _____

❽ 나타내다 _____

B 다음 장면에 어울리는 단어를 보기에서 골라 넣어 문장을 완성하세요.

bills	coins	When	money

1. I got some ⬚⬚⬚⬚⬚ from my mom.

2. I put the ⬚⬚⬚⬚⬚ in my piggy bank.*

3. I also put some ⬚⬚⬚⬚⬚ in, too.

4. ⬚⬚⬚⬚⬚ the piggy bank is full,

   I want to buy a doll.

＊**piggy bank** 돼지 저금통

C 빈칸에 알맞은 단어를 쓰고, 사다리를 타고 내려가 정답을 확인하세요.

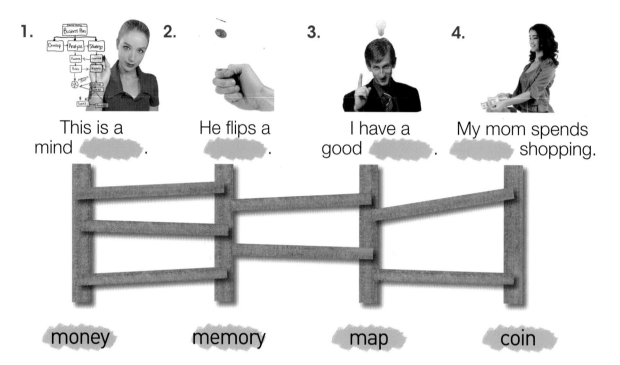

1. This is a mind _____ .

2. He flips a _____ .

3. I have a good _____ .

4. My mom spends _____ shopping.

money   memory   map   coin

D 문장을 읽고, 알맞은 단어에 동그라미 하세요.

1. The U.S. dollar is used all over the (word / world).
   미국 달러는 전세계에서 쓰인다.

2. We use it (where / when) we go abroad.
   우리는 외국에 갈 때 그것을 사용한다.

3. There are 7 kinds of (bills / kills) in U.S. dollars.
   미국 달러에는 7종류의 지폐가 있다.

4. I (selected / collected) all of them.   나는 그것들을 모두 수집했다.

5. I put them in my (scrapbook / sketchbook).
   나는 스크랩북에 그것들을 넣는다.

6. The bills (wrist / wrinkle) easily.   지폐는 쉽게 구겨진다.

7. Famous people's (paces / faces), like Washington's and Lincoln's, are on the bills.   워싱턴과 링컨 같은 유명한 사람들의 얼굴이 지폐에 있다.

8. They (represent / regard) the USA.   그들은 미국을 대표한다.

E 빈칸에 알맞은 단어를 단어 박스에서 찾아 넣어 이야기를 완성하세요.

Collecting Bills and Coins

This is my mo_____ collection.
I collect money w_____ I travel all over the _____.
I _____ money to remember my trips.

My coins are on my world _____. The _____ look different.
There are great people's _____ on the coins.
Things that r_____ each country are on the coins, too.
I tape* coins to my world map.

_____ are made of a special kind of paper.
There are pictures of important people and places on the bills, too.
I put them in a _____, so they will not get wr_____.
Whenever* I see my collection, I think about my _____ from
my trips. That makes me happy.

*tape 테이프로 붙이다 whenever ~할 때마다

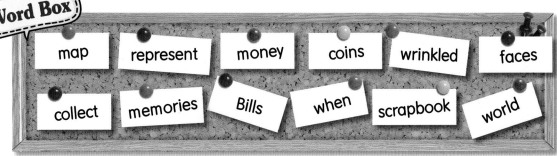

Word Box

map   represent   money   coins   wrinkled   faces

collect   memories   Bills   when   scrapbook   world

• Lesson 2 • Lucy's Nap with Her Dolls

1
✪ **with**
전 ~와 함께

with

2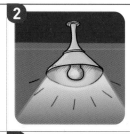
✪ **light**
명 빛, 조명
형 밝은

light

3
✪ **where**
부 어디에
접 ~한 곳에

where

4
✪ **always**
부 항상, 언제나
유 all the time 항상

always

5
✪ **cloudy**
형 구름이 낀, 흐린
명 cloud 구름

cloudy

6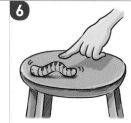
◯ **alive**
형 살아 있는
반 dead 죽은
동 live 살다

alive

7
◯ **prize**
명 상
유 award 상

prize

8
◯ **proud**
형 자랑스러운

proud

9
◯ **stage**
명 무대

stage

10
◯ **contest**
명 대회, 시합

contest

11
△ **hug**
동 껴안다, 포옹하다

hug

12
△ **nap**
명 낮잠

nap

A 우리말 뜻에 알맞은 단어를 쓰고, 크로스워드 퍼즐을 완성하세요.

▶▶▶ ACROSS

❶ 항상, 언제나 _____

❸ 낮잠 _____

❹ 껴안다 _____

❺ 대회 _____

❾ 어디에 _____

▼ DOWN

❷ ~와 함께 _____

❻ 자랑스러운 _____

❼ 빛, 조명 _____

❽ 무대 _____

B 연관되는 단어를 알아보고, 영어 또는 우리말 뜻을 쓰세요.

live		alive		dead
⑧ 살다	←	⑲ _____	↔	⑲ 죽은

prize		
⑲ _____	=	⑲ 상 _____

		cloudy
⑲ 구름 _____	←	⑲ _____

always		
⑼ _____	=	⑼ 항상 _____

C 동사 앞에 a-가 붙어 품사가 달라지는 단어를 알아보고, 빈칸에 알맞은 단어를 쓰세요.

> 동 live 살다 ◯ 형 alive 살아 있는
> 동 sleep 자다 ◯ 형 asleep 잠든

1. When I sing, I feel _____. 나는 노래할 때 살아있음을 느낀다.

2. He couldn't fall _____ because of the noise. 그는 소음 때문에 잠들 수 없었다.

3. What time do you go to _____? 너는 몇 시에 자니?

4. I _____ with my dog. 나는 개와 함께 산다.

D 문장을 읽고, 빈칸에 알맞은 단어를 쓰세요.

1. Kathy likes to dance _____ her friends.
   케이시는 친구들과 함께 춤추는 것을 좋아한다.

2. She also likes to dance on _____. 그녀는 또한 무대 위에서 춤추는 것을 좋아한다.

3. _____ are the dance festivals? 댄스 페스티벌은 어디에서 열리니?

4. Kathy _____ practices hard. 케이시는 항상 열심히 연습한다.

5. She even practices when her friends take _____.
   그녀는 친구들이 낮잠을 잘 때도 연습을 한다.

6. She takes part in a dance _____. 그녀는 댄스 대회에 참가한다.

7. When the _____ are on, she looks wonderful.
   조명들이 켜졌을 때, 그녀는 멋있어 보인다.

8. Finally, she wins a _____. 결국, 그녀는 상을 탄다.

9. She is happy. So, she _____ her dance partner.
   그녀는 행복하다. 그래서 그녀는 댄스 파트너를 껴안는다.

10. She is _____ of herself. 그녀는 자기 자신이 자랑스럽다.

Lucy's Nap with Her Dolls

Lucy's hobby is collecting Blythe dolls[*].

She likes playing _____ her dolls.

She a_____ brings them with her.

One day, she takes a _____ on the sofa.

She is h_____ her doll.

It's so cl_____ in her dream.

Suddenly, there is a l_____, but she can't open her eyes.

She can't believe _____ she is.

It's a Blythe doll modeling _____.

All the dolls are _____ and look wonderful.

Her favorite Blythe doll is on the _____.

She has long blond hair and beautiful green eyes.

She wins the first _____ and wears the crown.

She is the most beautiful Blythe doll in the world.

Lucy is so _____ of her.

When Lucy wakes up from the dream,
she finds the doll.

[*]**Blythe doll** (관절을 움직일 수 있고 눈의 색도 바꿀 수 있는, 머리가 큰) 블라이스 인형

Word Box

contest | with | where | always | stage | cloudy

light | hugging | alive | nap | prize | proud

Unit 2
Amazing B-Boy Dancers

★ 초등 기본어휘 ◇ 중등 기본어휘 ◆ 확장어휘

1

★ **hard**
- 튀 열심히
- 혱 어려운

hard

2

★ **dance**
- 동 춤추다 명 춤
- 명 dancer 춤추는 사람
- 혱 dancing 춤을 추는

dance

3

★ **every**
- 혱 모든, 매 ~마다
- 유 all, each 모든

every

4

★ **great**
- 혱 대단한, 훌륭한
- 유 wonderful, excellent 훌륭한

great

5

★ **another**
- 혱 또 하나의, 다른
- 유 other 다른

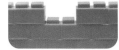

another

6

★ **pleased**
- 혱 기쁜
- 유 glad 기쁜

pleased

7

★ **give a big hand**
- 구 박수를 치다

give a big hand

8

◇ **spin**
- 동 회전하다, 돌다

spin

9

◇ **speed**
- 명 속도

speed

10

◇ **amazing**
- 혱 놀라운
- 유 surprising 놀라운

amazing

11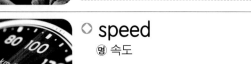

◇ **support**
- 동 지지하다, 떠받치다

support

12

◆ **teenager**
- 명 십대

teenager

A 우리말 뜻에 알맞은 단어를 쓰고, 크로스워드 퍼즐을 완성하세요.

▶▶▶ ACROSS

❷ 모든 _____

❹ 열심히 _____

❻ 속도 _____

❾ 또 하나의 _____

▼ DOWN

❶ 기쁜 _____

❸ 지지하다 _____

❺ 대단한 _____

❼ 회전하다 _____

❽ 십대 _____

B 다음 장면에 어울리는 단어를 보기에서 골라 넣어 문장을 완성하세요.

| speeds | spins | amazing | dances | teenager |

1. A B-boy _____ on the street.

2. He is a _____.

3. His dance is so _____.

4. He _____ at high _____.

C 빈칸에 알맞은 단어를 쓰고, 사다리를 타고 내려가 정답을 확인하세요.

1. I have _____ brother.

2. I study English _____.

3. He is _____ with the good score.

4. The _____ limit is 80 km an hour.

pleased   hard   speed   another

D 문장을 읽고, 알맞은 말에 동그라미 하세요.

1. I'm a (teenager / teenage) who likes to dance. 나는 춤추기를 좋아하는 십대이다.

2. A famous TV show holds a (drama / dance) contest.
   유명한 TV쇼에서 댄스 대회를 연다.

3. A dancer (spoils / spins) fast on the stage. 한 댄서가 무대에서 빨리 돈다.

4. (Every / All) dancer competes against each other. 모든 댄서들이 서로 경쟁한다.

5. I think they're all (great / ground) dancers.
   나는 그들이 모두 훌륭한 댄서라고 생각한다.

6. They perform (alive / amazing) dances. 그들은 놀라운 춤을 공연한다.

7. I (save / support) my favorite team. 나는 내가 가장 좋아하는 팀을 지지한다.

8. When they finish dancing, I (give them a big hand / get a big hand).
   그들이 춤추기를 끝낼 때, 나는 그들에게 큰 박수를 보낸다.

빈칸에 알맞은 단어를 단어 박스에서 찾아 넣어 이야기를 완성하세요.

Korean B-Boy Teams

Do you like B-boy _____?
B-boy dances are popular among t_____.

Look at the B-boy dancers!
They are really a_____.
One B-boy dancer s_____ at high _____.
A_____ B-boy dancer su_____ his body with only one arm.
Their dance is perfect.

People watch them dance and g_____ them _____
_____ _____. They practice really h_____.
Practice makes them perfect.

_____ year, the U.K. Championship* is held.
The Korean B-boy teams took part in the U.K. Championship.
They were so _____ that they won many prizes.
Many fans were _____ to hear about their success.

*the U.K. Championship 세계 4대 비보이 댄스 경연대회 중 하나

Word Box

| amazing | Another | give ~ a big hand | teenagers | dances | supports |

| pleased | speeds | Every | hard | spins | great |

• Lesson 2 • A B-Boy Prince

⭐ 초등 기본어휘 ◇ 중등 기본어휘 ⬢ 확장어휘

1
⭐ **pull**
동 당기다
반 push 밀다

pull

2
⭐ **role**
명 역할

role

3
⭐ **swim**
동 수영하다
명 swimming 수영

swim

4
⭐ **prince**
명 왕자
반 princess 공주

prince

5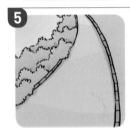
⭐ **street**
명 길, 거리
유 road, way 길, 거리

street

6
⭐ **handsome**
형 잘생긴
반 ugly 못생긴

handsome

7
⭐ **together**
부 함께, 같이
유 with ~와 함께

together

8
⭐ **go down on one's knees**
구 무릎을 꿇다

go down on one's knees

9
◇ **appear**
동 나타나다
반 disappear 사라지다

appear

10
◇ **partner**
명 동반자, 파트너

partner

11
◇ **perform**
동 공연하다
명 performance 공연

perform

12
⬢ **fantastic**
형 환상적인

fantastic

A 우리말 뜻에 알맞은 단어를 쓰고, 크로스워드 퍼즐을 완성하세요.

▶▶▶ ACROSS

❷ 역할 _____

❹ 환상적인 _____

❽ 당기다 _____

❿ 왕자 _____

▼ DOWN

❶ 동반자 _____

❸ 공연하다 _____

❺ 함께, 같이 _____

❻ 거리 _____

❼ 수영하다 _____

❾ 나타나다 _____

B 연관되는 단어를 알아보고, 영어 또는 우리말 뜻을 쓰세요.

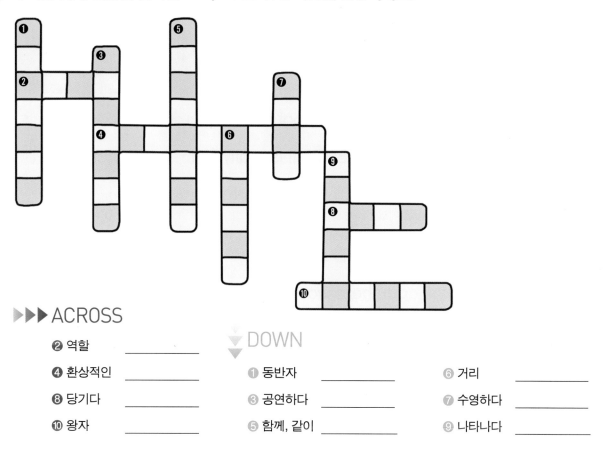

_____ = street = way
형 길, 거리   명 _____   명 길, 거리

pull   push
동 _____   동 밀다

handsome   _____
형 _____   형 못생긴

_____   appear
동 사라지다   동 _____

C 동사에 -ing를 붙여 명사를 만들 수 있어요. 빈칸에 알맞은 단어를 쓰세요.

> 통 **swim** 수영하다 ○ 명 **swimming** 수영
>
> 통 **run** 달리다 ○ 명 **running** 달리기

1. I like _____ in the pool. 나는 수영장에서 수영하는 것을 좋아한다.

2. _____ at the ABC Mall is really fun. ABC몰에서 쇼핑하는 것은 정말 재미있다.

3. I enjoy _____ in the park with my dog.
나는 나의 개와 함께 공원에서 달리는 것을 즐긴다.

D 문장을 읽고, 빈칸에 알맞은 단어를 쓰세요.

1. A long time ago, there was a boy who _____ a play.
오래 전에, 연극을 공연하는 소년이 있었다.

2. He performed a play with his dance partners on the _____.
그는 거리에서 댄스 파트너들과 연극을 공연했다.

3. One day, a _____ watched their play. 어느 날, 왕자가 그들의 연극을 보았다.

4. The boy _____ _____ on _____ _____.
그 소년은 무릎을 꿇었다.

5. "How about changing _____?" the prince said.
"역할들을 바꾸면 어떨까?" 왕자가 말했다.

6. The boy who became the prince looked _____.
왕자가 된 소년은 잘생겨 보였다.

7. The prince and the team performed the play _____.
왕자는 팀과 함께 연극을 공연했다.

8. They _____ and pushed each other while dancing.
그들은 춤을 추면서 서로 밀고 당겼다.

9. "It's _____ living outside the palace," the prince thought.
'궁전 밖에서 사는 것은 환상적이야.'라고 왕자는 생각했다.

10. A few days later, the boy _____, and they went back to their
own lives. 며칠 후, 소년이 나타났고, 그들은 자신들의 삶으로 돌아갔다.

E 빈칸에 알맞은 단어를 단어 박스에서 찾아 넣어 이야기를 완성하세요.

A B-Boy Prince

Lucy practices ballet at a ballet academy.

She is going to _____ Swan Lake.

She takes the _____ of Odette.

But she has no dance pa_____ yet.

One day, Lucy sees a s_____ dance performance.

The B-boy dancers dance really well.

It is amazing to watch their dance.

A h_____ B-boy dancer grabs Lucy's hand.

He _____ her up on stage.

Lucy dances on the stage with him.

Suddenly, she falls into a f_____ world.

The B-boy dancer changes into

a _____ and swims in the lake.

Lucy becomes a swan and sw_____ in the lake, too.

Suddenly, the handsome B-boy prince a_____.

He _____ _____ on one knee and proposes to her.

Then, Lucy becomes a beautiful princess.

They dance _____ under the moonlight.

Word Box

handsome	role	swims	together	fantastic	prince
appears	goes down	partner	street	perform	pulls

Unit 3
Murphy's Law

★ 초등 기본어휘 ◇ 중등 기본어휘 △ 확장어휘

1 ★ **call**
동 부르다

call

2 ★ **hour**
명 시간

hour

3 ★ **pass**
동 지나가다

pass

4 ★ **example**
명 예, 본보기
유 instance 예

example

5 ★ **problem**
명 문제
유 trouble 문제

problem

6 ★ **school bag**
명 책가방

school bag

7 ◇ **law**
명 법
유 rule 법, 규칙

law

8 ◇ **scold**
동 혼내다

scold

9 ◇ **decide**
동 결정하다
명 decision 결정

decide

10 ◇ **annoyed**
형 짜증이 나는, 화가 난
유 angry 화가 나는
동 annoy 성가시게 굴다

annoyed

11 △ **Coke**
명 콜라

Coke

12 △ **wallet**
명 지갑
유 purse 지갑

wallet

A 우리말 뜻에 알맞은 단어를 쓰고, 크로스워드 퍼즐을 완성하세요.

▶▶▶ ACROSS

❶ 부르다 _____

❸ 예, 본보기 _____

❻ 책가방 _____

❽ 콜라 _____

▼ DOWN

❷ 지갑 _____

❹ 짜증이 나는 _____

❺ 지나가다 _____

❼ 결정하다 _____

❾ 시간 _____

❿ 혼내다 _____

B 연관되는 단어를 알아보고, 영어 또는 우리말 뜻을 쓰세요.

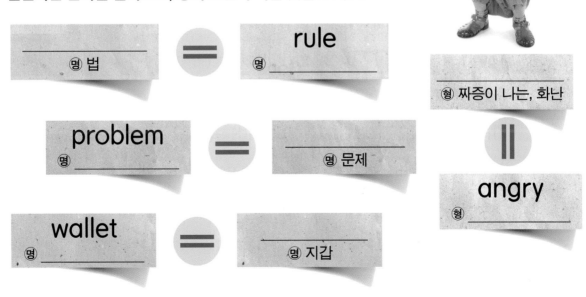

명 법 _____ = rule 명 _____

명 짜증이 나는, 화난

problem 명 _____ = 명 문제 _____

= angry 명 _____

wallet 명 _____ = 명 지갑 _____

C 빈칸에 알맞은 단어를 쓰고, 사다리를 타고 내려가 정답을 확인하세요.

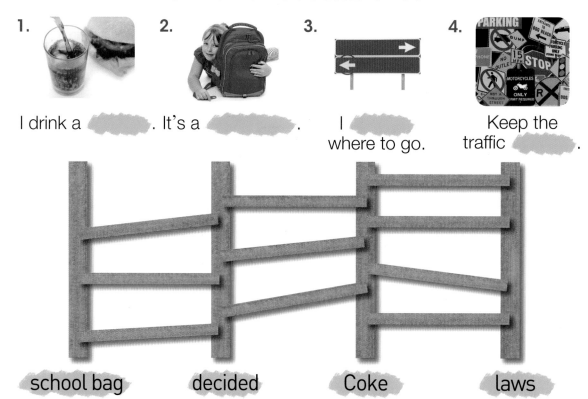

1. I drink a _____ .

2. It's a _____ .

3. I _____ where to go.

4. Keep the traffic _____ .

school bag   decided   Coke   laws

D 문장을 읽고, 알맞은 말에 동그라미 하세요.

1. This is an (example / show) of Murphy's Law.   이것은 머피의 법칙의 예이다.

2. Tom had a (pain / problem) this morning.   톰은 오늘 아침에 문제가 있었다.

3. He left his (watch / wallet) at home.   그는 집에 지갑을 두고 왔다.

4. The school bus (passed / crashed) by him.   학교 버스가 그의 옆을 지나갔다.

5. At school, the teacher (called / joined) the roll.   학교에서 선생님이 출석을 부르셨다.

6. He was an (minute / hour) late.   그는 한 시간 지각했다.

7. The teacher (scolded / shouted) him.   선생님이 그를 꾸짖으셨다.

8. He was (annoying / annoyed).   그는 짜증이 났다.

E 빈칸에 알맞은 단어를 단어 박스에서 찾아 넣어 이야기를 완성하세요.

The Meaning of Murphy's Law

Do you know Murphy's _____?
When anything that can go wrong does go wrong,
we c_____ this Murphy's Law.
Let me give you some _____.
– You wait for the bus for an _____,
but it doesn't arrive.
You _____ to take a taxi.
But as soon as you get in it, the bus _____ by.
This is Murphy's Law.
– You lose your w_____ and buy a new one.
Then you find it in your s_____ _____.
This is Murphy's Law.
– Your mom _____ you for something
you didn't do, so you are a_____.
You kick a can of _____.
It hits a police officer's head
and you have some _____.
This is Murphy's Law.

Word Box

school bag · call · decide · hour · examples · passes

Coke · Law · problems · annoyed · wallet · scolds

•Lesson 2• An Unlucky Day

✪ 초등 기본어휘 ◇ 중등 기본어휘 △ 확장어휘

1

✪ **miss**
동 놓치다

miss

2

I'm late.

✪ **hurry**
동 서두르다
유 rush 서두르다

hurry

3

✪ **wrong**
형 틀린
반 right 옳은

wrong

4

✪ **office**
명 사무실, 회사

office

5

✪ **unlucky**
형 운이 없는
반 lucky 행운의

unlucky

6

✪ **fall on one's face**
구 앞으로 넘어지다

fall on one's face

7

◇ **reach**
동 도착하다
유 arrive 도착하다

reach

8

◇ **barely**
부 간신히

barely

9

◇ **balance**
명 균형

balance

10

◇ **mechanic**
명 정비공

mechanic

11

◇ **suddenly**
부 갑자기
명 형 sudden 갑작스러움;
갑작스러운

suddenly

12

△ **wedding**
명 결혼(식)

wedding

A 우리말 뜻에 알맞은 단어를 쓰고, 크로스워드 퍼즐을 완성하세요.

▶▶▶ACROSS

❶ 갑자기 _____

❷ 틀린 _____

❹ 도착하다 _____

❺ 운이 없는 _____

❻ 간신히 _____

❽ 놓치다 _____

▼ DOWN

❸ 결혼(식) _____

❻ 균형 _____

❼ 서두르다 _____

❽ 정비공 _____

B 다음 장면에 어울리는 단어를 보기에서 골라 넣어 문장을 완성하세요.

| unlucky | office | balance | fell on his face |

1. He went out of his _____.

2. He lost his _____ on the stair.

3. He _____.

4. It was an _____ day.

C 우리말 뜻에 맞는 형용사 또는 부사를 빈칸에 쓰세요.

> It is a <u>sudden</u> change. It changes <u>suddenly</u>.
> 형 sudden 갑작스러운 　　　　　　 부 suddenly 갑자기
> It was <u>unlucky</u> that I failed. <u>Unluckily</u>, I failed.
> 형 unlucky 운이 없는 　　　　　　 부 unluckily 불행히도

1. It was a _____ death. 그것은 갑작스러운 죽음이었다.

2. He died _____. 그는 갑자기 죽었다.

3. It was an _____ exam. 그것은 운이 없는 시험이었다.

4. _____, I have an exam. 불행히도 나는 시험이 있다.

D 문장을 읽고, 빈칸에 알맞은 말을 쓰세요.

1. Nancy's uncle is a _____. 낸시의 삼촌은 기계공이다.

2. He doesn't work at the _____. He works at the garage.
   그는 사무실에서 일하지 않는다. 그는 정비소에서 일한다.

3. He's going to a _____ this afternoon. 오늘 오후에 그는 결혼식에 갈 것이다.

4. He _____ to get dressed. 그는 서둘러서 옷을 입는다.

5. He _____ the bus to the garage. 그는 정비소에 가는 버스를 놓친다.

6. What's _____? The bus passed by. 뭐가 잘못된 걸까? 버스가 지나갔다.

7. He loses his _____. 그는 중심을 잃는다.

8. He _____ on _____ _____.
   그는 앞으로 넘어진다.

9. He can _____ stand up. 그는 간신히 일어난다.

10. He _____ the garage on time. 그는 제시간에 정비소에 도착한다.

E 빈칸에 알맞은 단어를 단어 박스에서 찾아 넣어 이야기를 완성하세요.

An Unlucky Day

Lucy's aunt has a w_____ today.

Lucy's father doesn't go to the o_____.

Lucy and her family go to the wedding.

Lucy's father starts the engine but it doesn't work.

"What's _____ with the car? We should call a me_____."

When the mechanic arrives, the car starts by itself.

Vroom, vroom. Her father rushes to the wedding.

"_____ up, or we will _____ the wedding!"

_____, a car hits Lucy's car.

"Ahhhh! We will be late for the wedding!"

They r_____ the wedding just in time.

"We b_____ made it. Come on. Run, run!"

Lucy steps on her long dress and loses her _____.

She falls flat _____ _____ _____.

"Oh, my god! What an _____ day!"

Word Box

wedding · unlucky · wrong · office · Hurry · mechanic

Suddenly · miss · balance · barely · reach · on her face

Unit 4
Mom's Words

To My Lovely Daughter

✪ 초등 기본어휘   ◯ 중등 기본어휘   △ 확장어휘

1
✪ **hope**
동 바라다
명 희망
유 want, wish 바라다

hope

2
✪ **word**
명 말, 낱말, 단어

word

3
✪ **knock**
동 (문을) 두드리다

knock

4
✪ **future**
명 미래
반 past 과거

future

5
✪ **honest**
형 정직한
반 dishonest 정직하지 않은

honest

6
✪ **come true**
구 실현되다

come true

7
◯ **healthy**
형 건강한, 건강에 좋은
반 unhealthy 건강하지 않은
명 health 건강

healthy

8
◯ **regularly**
부 규칙적으로
반 irregularly 불규칙하게

regularly

9
◯ **various**
형 다양한
유 diverse 다양한

various

10
◯ **postpone**
동 뒤로 미루다
유 put off 뒤로 미루다

postpone

11
◯ **challenge**
동 시도하다
명 도전

challenge

12
◯ **important**
형 중요한
명 importance 중요성

important

A 우리말 뜻에 알맞은 단어를 쓰고, 크로스워드 퍼즐을 완성하세요.

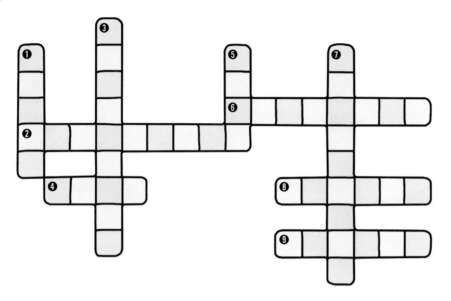

▶▶▶ ACROSS

❷ 도전하다 _____

❹ 말, 낱말, 단어 _____

❻ 뒤로 미루다 _____

❽ 미래 _____

❾ 정직한 _____

▼ DOWN

❶ (문을) 두드리다 _____

❸ 규칙적으로 _____

❺ 바라다; 희망 _____

❼ 중요한 _____

B 다음 장면에 어울리는 단어를 보기에서 골라 넣어 문장을 완성하세요.

important　　regularly　　various　　healthy

1. There are _____ kinds of food.

2. These are _____ foods.

3. Try to eat _____ for your health.

4. It's _____ for us to eat 3 meals a day.

빈칸에 알맞은 단어를 쓰고, 사다리를 타고 내려가 정답을 확인하세요.

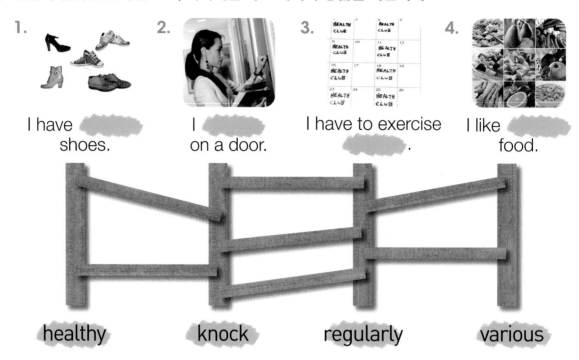

1. I have _____ shoes.

2. I _____ on a door.

3. I have to exercise _____.

4. I like _____ food.

healthy   knock   regularly   various

D 문장을 읽고, 알맞은 단어에 동그라미 하세요.

1. I think about my (future / past). 나는 미래에 대해 생각한다.

2. I want to be a famous cook. My dream will (come true / come back).
   나는 유명한 요리사가 되고 싶다. 나의 꿈은 이루어질 것이다.

3. My parents say, "We (tell / hope) you will be a famous cook in the future." 부모님은 "네가 장차 유명한 요리사가 되길 바란다."라고 말씀하신다.

4. They also say, "We want you to (challenge / chase) yourself to try new things." 부모님은 또한 말씀하신다. "우리는 네가 새로운 일들에 도전해 보길 바란다."

5. I listen to my parents' (wishes / words). 나는 부모님 말씀을 듣는다.

6. I think that it is (important / difficult) to read many books about my dreams. 나는 내 꿈에 관한 많은 책을 읽는 것이 중요하다고 생각한다.

7. I shouldn't (postpone / help) what I have to do. 나는 해야 할 일을 뒤로 미루지 말아야 한다.

8. I do my best to be (kind / honest) when I make meals.
   나는 음식을 만들 때 정직하려고 최선을 다한다.

To My Lovely Daughter

My daughter, Lily.

I love you very much.

So I'll tell you something i _____.

Please listen to my _____.

I want you to have big dreams for your _____.

I really want your dreams to _____ _____.

And I want you to be h_____.

I want you to exercise r_____.

I want you to read _____ books.

I want you to ch_____ yourself.

Do what you have never done before.

And be _____. Don't tell lies.

_____ on the door before you enter another person's room.

I really _____ that you live a happy life.

Oh, one more thing.

Please don't _____ what you have to do.

From Mom

Word Box

important words honest come true hope regularly

future various healthy challenge postpone Knock

✪ 초등 기본어휘 ◇ 중등 기본어휘 △ 확장어휘

1

✪ **read**
⟮동⟯ 읽다

read

2

✪ **wait**
⟮동⟯ 기다리다

wait

3

✪ **wash**
⟮동⟯ 씻다
⟮형⟯ washable 물세탁 가능한

wash

4
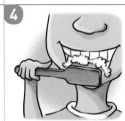
✪ **brush**
⟮동⟯ (솔로) 닦다
⟮명⟯ 솔

brush

5

✪ **homework**
⟮명⟯ 숙제

homework

6

✪ **make a bed**
⟮구⟯ 잠자리를 정돈하다

make a bed

7

◇ **comb**
⟮동⟯ 빗질하다
⟮명⟯ 머리빗

comb

8

◇ **share**
⟮동⟯ 함께 쓰다

share

9

◇ **exercise**
⟮동⟯ 운동하다
⟮명⟯ 운동

exercise

10
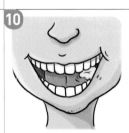
△ **chew**
⟮동⟯ 씹다

chew

11

◇ **nagging**
⟮명⟯ 잔소리
⟮형⟯ 잔소리가 심한
⟮동⟯ nag 잔소리를 하다

nagging

12

◇ **oversleep**
⟮동⟯ 늦잠 자다

oversleep

A 우리말 뜻에 알맞은 단어를 쓰고, 크로스워드 퍼즐을 완성하세요.

▶▶▶ACROSS

❷ (솔로) 닦다 _____

❸ 잔소리 _____

❹ 읽다 _____

❺ 늦잠 자다 _____

❼ 기다리다 _____

▼ DOWN

❶ 빗질하다 _____

❻ 함께 쓰다 _____

❼ 씻다 _____

❽ 운동하다 _____

❾ 숙제 _____

B 빈칸을 완성하고, 나의 소망 목록과 엄마의 잔소리 목록을 선으로 연결해 보세요.

I want to r_____ comic books.

I want to play computer games.

Do your h_____.

Mom's nagging

my wish list

W_____ your hands.

I usually o_____.

M_____ your bed.

C wait에 대해 알아보고, 빈칸에 알맞은 말을 쓰세요.

> **wait to** + 동사원형: ~하기 위해 기다리다
> ex I <u>wait to</u> play outside. 나는 밖에서 놀기 위해 기다린다.
> **wait for**: ~을 기다리다
> ex He <u>waits for</u> me. 그는 나를 기다린다.

1. I _____ to see a doctor. 나는 의사 선생님을 만나기 위해 기다린다.

2. She waits _____ buy a book. 그녀는 책을 사기 위해 기다린다.

3. He _____ _____ a train. 그는 기차를 기다린다.

D 문장을 읽고, 빈칸에 알맞은 단어를 쓰세요.

1. My friends and I go camping. But we _____.
   친구들과 나는 캠프를 간다. 그러나 우리는 늦잠을 잔다.

2. The teacher says, "_____ your _____ quickly."
   선생님이 말씀하신다. "빨리 이부자리를 정리해라."

3. I want to _____ my face. 나는 세수를 하고 싶다.

4. We think about our vacation _____ at camp.
   우리는 캠프에서 방학숙제에 관해 생각한다.

5. I _____ a bathroom with my friends. 나는 친구들과 욕실을 함께 쓴다.

6. My friend Paul _____ his teeth in the bathroom.
   친구 폴이 욕실에서 양치질을 한다.

7. He also _____ his hair slowly. 폴은 또 머리를 천천히 빗는다.

8. I am _____ him to hurry up. 나는 그에게 서두르라고 잔소리를 하고 있다.

9. I _____ my food slowly. 나는 음식을 천천히 씹는다.

10. Paul _____ a newspaper in bed. 폴은 침대에서 신문을 읽는다.

11. The newspaper says, "_____ every morning. It is good for you."
    '매일 아침 운동을 하세요. 당신에게 좋습니다.'라고 신문에 쓰여 있다.

E 빈칸에 알맞은 단어를 단어 박스에서 찾아 넣어 이야기를 완성하세요.

Mom's Nagging

Today is Sunday. Lucy is sleeping.

Lucy's mom is _____ Lucy.

"Don't o_____."

"_____ your face."

"_____ your teeth."

"_____ your hair."

"_____ your _____."

"Don't eat too much fast food. Ch_____ slowly."

"_____ every day to be healthy."

"_____ many books."

"_____ your things with your friends."

"W_____ your turn."

"Do your _____."

"What are you going to do first?"

Lucy says, "Ah~ I'm tired of my mom's nagging.

I want to live in a world where there's no nagging."

Word Box

homework　　Read　　Brush　　Exercise　　Wash　　nagging

oversleep　　Comb　　Make ~ bed　　Share　　Wait　　Chew

Unit 5
Bookworm

★ 초등 기본어휘 ◐ 중등 기본어휘 ◯ 확장어휘

1

★ **get**
동 받다, 얻다

get

2

★ **best**
형 가장 좋은 명 최고
원 good 좋은 비 better 더 좋은
반 worst 최악의

best

3

★ **some**
형 약간의, 얼마간의

some

4

★ **check**
동 확인하다

check

5

★ **right**
부 곧장, 곧바로

right

6

★ **choose**
동 선택하다
명 choice 선택

choose

7

◐ **vote**
동 투표하다
유 poll 투표하다

vote

8

◐ **award**
명 상
유 prize 상

award

9

◯ **fiction**
명 소설, 꾸며낸 이야기
반 nonfiction 비소설

fiction

10

◯ **bookmark**
명 책갈피

bookmark

11

◯ **bookworm**
명 책벌레, 독서광

bookworm

12

◯ **book report**
명 독후감, 독서 감상문

book report

A 우리말 뜻에 알맞은 단어를 쓰고, 크로스워드 퍼즐을 완성하세요.

▶▶▶ ACROSS

❶ 상 　＿＿＿＿＿＿

❷ 가장 좋은; 최고 　＿＿＿＿＿＿

❺ 선택하다 　＿＿＿＿＿＿

❻ 확인하다 　＿＿＿＿＿＿

❼ 투표하다 　＿＿＿＿＿＿

❽ 책벌레, 독서광 　＿＿＿＿＿＿

▼ DOWN

❸ 받다, 얻다 　＿＿＿＿＿＿

❹ 곧장, 곧바로 　＿＿＿＿＿＿

❾ 독후감 　＿＿＿＿＿＿

❿ 책갈피 　＿＿＿＿＿＿

⓫ 약간의 　＿＿＿＿＿＿

B 다음 장면에 어울리는 단어를 보기에서 골라 넣어 문장을 완성하세요.

some	fiction	bookworm	book report

1. I am a ⬚⬚⬚⬚⬚ .

2. I read ⬚⬚⬚⬚⬚ books every day.

3. I like to read both ⬚⬚⬚⬚⬚ and nonfiction.

4. I write a ⬚⬚⬚⬚⬚ after reading each book.

C 빈칸에 알맞은 단어를 쓰고, 사다리를 타고 내려가 정답을 확인하세요.

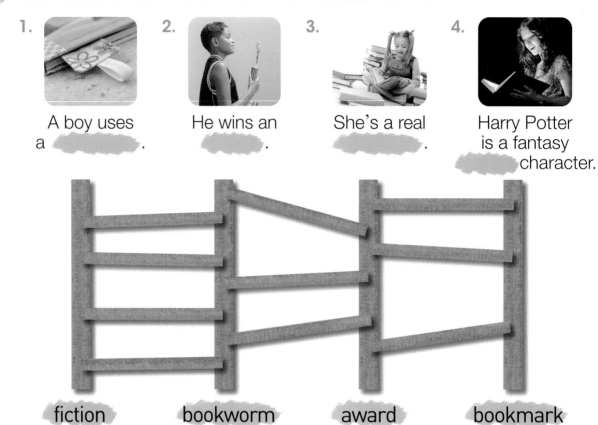

1. A boy uses a _____.

2. He wins an _____.

3. She's a real _____.

4. Harry Potter is a fantasy _____ character.

fiction   bookworm   award   bookmark

D 문장을 읽고, 알맞은 단어에 동그라미 하세요.

1. What is the (best / worst) book this year?
   올해의 최고의 책은 무엇일까?

2. Children (wait / vote) for it.   아이들이 투표를 한다.

3. They (choose / read) *The Lord of the Rings*.   아이들은 '반지의 제왕'을 선택한다.

4. Children write (comic books / book reports).   아이들은 독서 감상문을 쓴다.

5. A writer (checks / changes) them carefully.   작가는 그것들을 꼼꼼하게 체크한다.

6. The writer wrote (some / any) mystery novels.   그 작가는 추리소설 몇 편을 썼다.

7. The winner (gets / makes) a prize.   우승자는 상을 받는다.

8. Come (far / right) away and collect your prize.   바로 와서 상을 받아라.

Children's Book Awards

It's time for the Children's Book _____ .

Go to the school library and c_____e the book you like the b_____ .

What's your favorite book?

C_____ your favorite book.

V_____ for the best book.

- _____
  - *James and the Giant Peach, Charlotte's Web, Harry Potter*
- **Nonfiction**
  - *The Diary of Anne Frank, The Great Invention, The Seven Habits of Happy Kids*

There are also _____ wonderful activities.

You can meet writers and _____ autographs[*]

You can make your own b_____ .

You can share your _____ _____ with your friends.

Then we'll give a prize to the _____ who reads over 10 books a month.

Please come _____ away!

*autograph 사인

Word Box

bookworm　Check　best　choose　some　Fiction

Vote　get　bookmark　right　Awards　book report

A Gift from Harry

✪ 초등 기본어휘 ◇ 중등 기본어휘 △ 확장어휘

1
✪ fan
명 팬

fan

2
✪ dark
명 어둠
형 어두운
반 light 빛; 밝은

dark

3
✪ hold
동 잡다
유 grasp 붙잡다

hold

4
✪ spell
명 주문
동 주문을 외우다

spell

5
✪ voice
명 목소리

voice

6
✪ ask for
구 ~을 요청하다, ~을 부탁하다

ask for

7
✪ become
동 ~이 되다

become

8
✪ mirror
명 거울

mirror

9
◇ rush
동 돌진하다

rush

10
◇ brave
형 용감한
유 courageous 용감한

brave

11
△ dragon
명 용

dragon

12
△ wizard
명 마법사
유 witch 마녀

wizard

A 우리말 뜻에 알맞은 단어를 쓰고, 크로스워드 퍼즐을 완성하세요.

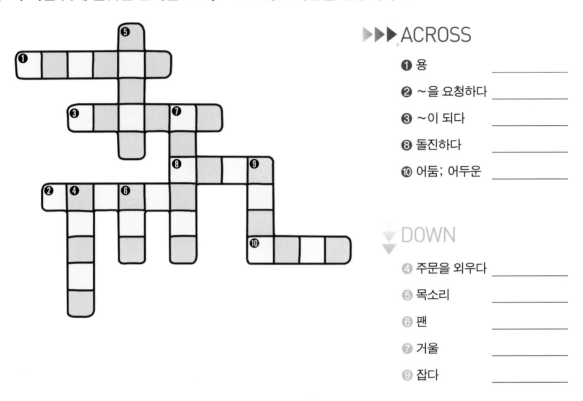

▶▶▶ACROSS

❶ 용 _____

❷ ~을 요청하다 _____

❸ ~이 되다 _____

❽ 돌진하다 _____

❿ 어둠; 어두운 _____

▼ DOWN

❹ 주문을 외우다 _____

❺ 목소리 _____

❻ 팬 _____

❼ 거울 _____

❾ 잡다 _____

B 연관되는 단어를 알아보고, 영어 또는 우리말 뜻을 쓰세요.

(형) 용감한 = courageous (형) _____

(명) 어둠 ↔ light (명) _____

wizard (명) _____ = witch (명) _____

(동) 잡다 _____ = grasp (동) _____

C ask와 ask for의 사용법에 대해 알아보고, 빈칸에 알맞은 말을 쓰세요.

> **ask** 묻다, 질문하다
> ex I <u>ask</u> him a question.   나는 그에게 질문을 한다.
> **ask for** ~을 요청하다, ~을 부탁하다
> ex I <u>ask for</u> some money.   나는 돈을 좀 부탁한다.

1. She _____ the way to the hospital.   그녀는 병원 가는 길을 묻는다.

2. He _____ me nothing.   그는 나에게 아무것도 묻지 않는다.

3. I _____ _____ his help to clean the room.
    나는 그에게 방을 치우는 데 도움을 달라고 부탁한다.

4. She _____ me _____ a special gift.
    그녀는 나에게 특별한 선물을 요구한다.

D 문장을 읽고, 빈칸에 알맞은 단어를 쓰세요.

1. Jessie is a _____ and bright girl.   제시는 용감하고 영리한 소녀이다.

2. She is a big _____ of Harry.   그녀는 해리의 열광적인 팬이다.

3. Harry is a famous _____.   해리는 유명한 마법사이다.

4. He has a nice _____.   그는 멋진 목소리를 가졌다.

5. One day, a _____ comes to the town.   어느 날, 용이 마을에 나타난다.

6. It gets Harry under its _____.   그것이 해리에게 주문을 건다.

7. It puts him in a magic _____.   그것이 그를 요술 거울에 가둔다.

8. Harry fears the _____.   해리는 어둠을 무서워한다.

9. Jessie _____ into the magic mirror.   제시는 요술 거울로 돌진한다.

10. She _____ the dragon with a rope.   그녀는 밧줄로 용을 붙잡는다.

11. Jessie _____ Harry's heroine.   제시는 해리의 영웅이 된다.

빈칸에 알맞은 단어를 단어 박스에서 찾아 넣어 이야기를 완성하세요.

A Gift from Harry

Lucy loves to read *Harry Potter*.

One night, a white owl appears in her m_____.

Lucy _____ the owl _____ help.

"Can you take me to Hogwarts?" Lucy falls into the mirror.

Lucy meets Harry, so she _____ excited.

"I'm your biggest _____. How can I become a w_____?"

Harry says, "Shh, don't speak in a loud _____. Come with me."

Harry opens the door in the d_____.

A _____ is flying in the night sky.

He says the spell, "Incendio, locomoter."

A fire starts, and it r_____ into the dragon's mouth.

Lucy says, "You are so br_____. I want to learn your s_____."

Harry says, "Let me give you this spell list."

Lucy wakes up _____ a spell book in her hand.

Lucy goes out and shouts, "Incendio!"

Word Box

fan   brave   wizard   mirror   becomes   voice

dark   holding   dragon   asks ~ for   rushes   spells

Unit 6
About Cars

☆ 초등 기본어휘 ◇ 중등 기본어휘 ⏶ 확장어휘

1 ☆ **low**
형 낮은
반 high 높은

low

2  ☆ **rich**
형 부자인
반 poor 가난한

rich

3  ☆ **cheap**
형 싼
반 expensive 비싼

cheap

4 ☆ **first**
형 처음의

first

5 ☆ **price**
명 가격

price

6 ☆ **middle class**
명 중간 계층, 중산층

middle class

7  ◇ **mass**
형 대중의, 많은 양의

mass

8  ◇ **effect**
명 영향, 효과

effect

9  ◇ **system**
명 방식, 시스템

system

10 ◇ **quality**
명 질

quality

11  ◇ **produce**
동 제작하다, 만들다

produce

12 ⏶ **slogan**
명 표어

slogan

A 우리말 뜻에 알맞은 단어를 쓰고, 크로스워드 퍼즐을 완성하세요.

▶▶▶ ACROSS

❶ 중산층 _____

❸ 방식 _____

❺ 싼 _____

❻ 질 _____

❽ 생산하다 _____

▼ DOWN

❷ 처음의 _____

❹ 영향 _____

❼ 가격 _____

❾ 부자인 _____

❿ 표어 _____

B 빈칸에 알맞은 단어를 쓰고, 연관되는 단어끼리 선으로 연결하세요.

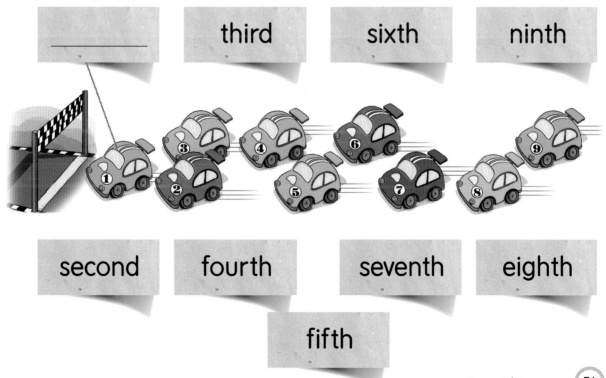

third   sixth   ninth

second   fourth   seventh   eighth

fifth

1. It's a _____ mountain.

2. I'm _____.

3. I like this poster _____.

4. This is my _____ bike.

rich   slogan   low   first

D 문장을 읽고, 알맞은 단어에 동그라미 하세요.

1. Radio is one form of (mass / many) media. 라디오는 대중 매체의 한 형태이다.

2. People say that the radio advertisement (style / system) is old.
사람들은 라디오 광고 시스템이 낡았다고 말한다.

3. However, the (high class / middle class) listens to the radio a lot.
그러나 중산층은 라디오를 많이 듣는다.

4. The (emotion / effect) of radio advertisements is great.
라디오 광고의 효과는 대단하다.

5. I (present / produce) a variety of advertisements. 나는 다양한 라디오 광고를 만든다.

6. The (quality / quantity) of my advertisements is high. 내 광고의 질은 좋다.

7. The (price / prince) of the advertisements is quite good.
그 광고들의 가격은 꽤 괜찮다.

8. Actually, it's really (change / cheap). 사실, 그것은 정말 싸다.

Ford Model T

Watch the Ford go by.

"HIGH Q_____ IN A _____-PRICED CAR"

This was the poster _____ of the Ford Model T in 1909.

Henry Ford _____ the Ford Model T from 1908 to 1927.

Ford made the car with a new s_____, the assembly line*.

The Ford Model T was the first car _____-produced on an assembly line.

It was so _____ that ordinary people could afford it.

Before the Ford Model T, the _____ of cars were very expensive.

So only _____ people could buy cars at that time.

After the Ford Model T, cars became popular.

The car made traveling easy for _____ _____ Americans.

Ford had an important e_____ on people's lives.

That's why the Model T is called

"the _____ people's car."

*assembly line 조립라인

Word Box

first   prices   effect   mass   cheap   slogan

produced   rich   system   middle class   LOW   QUALITY

A Flying Car

✪ 초등 기본어휘 ◇ 중등 기본어휘 ◬ 확장어휘

1
✪ **far**
혱 (거리가) 먼
뺀 near 가까운

far

2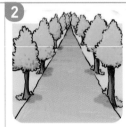
✪ **road**
뎽 길
윦 street 길

road

3
✪ **really**
믠 정말, 진짜

really

4
✪ **at last**
권 마침내
윦 finally 마침내

at last

5
✪ **get in[on]**
권 (차를) 타다
get in the car 차를 타다
get on the bus 버스를 타다

get in[on]

6
✪ **airplane**
뎽 비행기

airplane

7
✪ **traffic jam**
뎽 교통혼잡

traffic jam

8
◇ **stick**
둉 끼어들게 하다, 꼼짝 못하다
뎽 막대기

stick

9
◇ **shake**
둉 흔들다

shake

10
◇ **severe**
혱 엄한, 심한

severe

11
◇ **happen**
둉 (사건이) 일어나다

happen

12
◬ **dizzy**
혱 어지러운

dizzy

A 우리말 뜻에 알맞은 단어를 쓰고, 크로스워드 퍼즐을 완성하세요.

▶▶▶ ACROSS

❷ 비행기 _____

❺ 꼼짝 못하다 _____

❼ 엄한, 심한 _____

❿ 어지러운 _____

▼ DOWN

❶ (거리가) 먼 _____

❸ 정말, 진짜 _____

❹ 마침내 _____

❻ 흔들다 _____

❽ (차를) 타다 _____

❾ 길 _____

B 다음 장면에 어울리는 단어를 보기에서 골라 넣어 문장을 완성하세요.

happened	get on	traffic jam

1. There is a _____ .

2. What _____ ?
   There was a car accident.

3. You had better _____ the subway.

C 과거형 동사에 대해 알아보고, 빈칸에 알맞은 과거형 동사를 쓰세요.

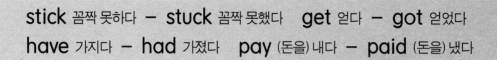

> stick 꼼짝 못하다 – stuck 꼼짝 못했다   get 얻다 – got 얻었다
> have 가지다 – had 가졌다   pay (돈을) 내다 – paid (돈을) 냈다

1. He's _____ on the road.   그는 길에서 꼼짝 못하게 되었다.

2. I _____ a great time on my birthday.   내 생일에 나는 좋은 시간을 가졌다.

3. My mom _____ for the food at the supermarket.
   우리 엄마는 슈퍼마켓에서 그 음식 값을 냈다.

4. David _____ a new cell phone.   데이비드는 새로운 휴대전화를 얻었다.

D 문장을 읽고, 빈칸에 알맞은 단어를 쓰세요.

1. Mom _____ me and says, "Wake up!"   엄마가 나를 흔들며 말한다. "일어나!"

2. Oh! I'm late. But the traffic jam is _____.
   앗! 지각이다. 그런데 교통체증이 심각하다.

3. My school is _____ from my house.   학교는 우리 집에서 멀다.

4. I have to cross the _____ and get on the bus.
   나는 길을 건너서 버스를 타야 한다.

5. I want to go to school by _____ every morning.
   나는 아침마다 비행기를 타고 학교에 가고 싶다.

6. _____ _____, the bus is coming.   마침내, 버스가 온다.

7. I _____ on the bus.   나는 버스에 탄다.

8. My skirt gets _____ in the door.   치마가 문에 낀다.

9. I'm so embarrassed and I feel _____.   나는 너무 부끄러워서 어지럽기까지 하다.

10. I _____ want to get off the bus.   나는 정말 버스에서 내리고 싶다.

E 빈칸에 알맞은 단어를 단어 박스에서 찾아 넣어 이야기를 완성하세요.

A Flying Car

Many cars are on the _____.

"There's a _____ _____. It's s_____.

We're _____ on the road," says Lucy's dad.

"We're too _____ from home.

I need a flying car. Abracadabra!" says Lucy.

Then, a flying car lands on the road.

Lucy and her dad _____ in the flying car.

The flying car flies up into the sky.

However, the flying car begins to sh_____.

"Dad, what is _____? I feel _____."

"Lucy, don't worry. An _____ flew past us."

_____ _____, they arrive at home.

"Wow! We're home. That was r_____ fast!"

Word Box

| road | At last | severe | traffic jam | get | airplane |

| far | stuck | really | happening | dizzy | shake |

Unit 7
At the Beach

• Lesson 1 • *Boracay Beach*

✪ 초등 기본어휘　◇ 중등 기본어휘　△ 확장어휘

1

✪ **fat**
형 뚱뚱한
반 thin 마른

fat

2

✪ **sell**
동 팔다
명 sale 판매

sell

3

✪ **beach**
명 해변
유 seashore 해변

beach

4

✪ **relax**
동 휴식을 취하다
유 rest 쉬다

relax

5

✪ **visitor**
명 손님, 방문객
유 guest 손님

visitor

6

✪ **water fight**
명 물싸움

water fight

7

◇ **lie**
동 눕다, 거짓말하다
명 거짓말

lie

8

◇ **view**
명 경치, 경관
유 scene 경치

view

9

◇ **along**
부 ~을 따라서

along

10

◇ **shallow**
형 얕은
반 deep 깊은

shallow

11

◇ **sandcastle**
명 모래성

sandcastle

12

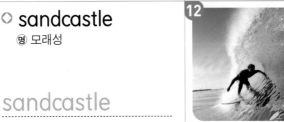

△ **surf**
동 파도타기를 하다
명 surfer 파도타기 하는 사람

surf

A

우리말 뜻에 알맞은 단어를 쓰고, 크로스워드 퍼즐을 완성하세요.

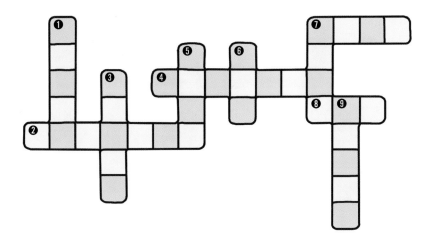

▶▶▶ ACROSS

❷ 얕은 _____

❹ 손님, 방문객 _____

❼ 팔다 _____

❽ 뚱뚱한 _____

▼ DOWN

❶ 해변 _____

❸ 휴식을 취하다 _____

❺ 경치, 경관 _____

❻ 눕다; 거짓말 _____

❼ 파도타기를 하다 _____

❾ ~을 따라서 _____

B

다음 장면에 어울리는 단어를 보기에서 골라 넣어 문장을 완성하세요.

| beach | water fights | surfs | sandcastles |

1. People go to the _____ in summer.

2. Some people build _____.

3. A man _____ in the sea.

4. Kids have _____ on the beach.

C 빈칸에 알맞은 단어를 쓰고, 사다리를 타고 내려가 정답을 확인하세요.

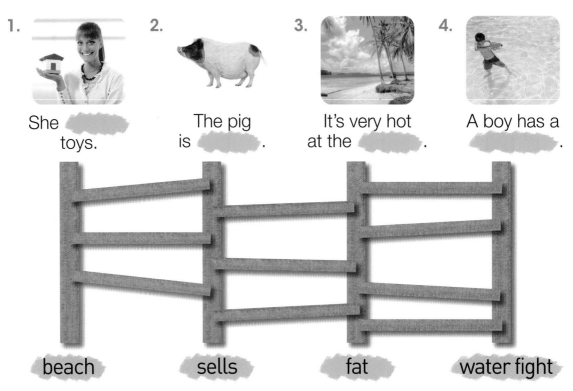

1. She _____ toys.

2. The pig is _____.

3. It's very hot at the _____.

4. A boy has a _____.

beach   sells   fat   water fight

D 문장을 읽고, 알맞은 단어에 동그라미 하세요.

1. We (relax / exercise) at the resort in summer.   우리는 여름에는 리조트에서 쉰다.

2. The resort is full of (students / visitors).   그 리조트는 많은 방문객들로 꽉 차있다.

3. We stay in a room with a nice (view / watch).   우리는 전망 좋은 방에 머문다.

4. We walk (around / along) the beach near the resort.
   우리는 리조트 근처에 있는 바닷가를 따라 걷는다.

5. Many men learn how to (sell / surf) at the beach.
   많은 남자들이 해변에서 파도타기를 배운다.

6. Children swim in the (shallow / show) water at the beach.
   아이들은 해변의 얕은 물에서 수영을 한다.

7. Many people (fall / lie) on the beach.   많은 사람들이 해변 위에 누워 있다.

8. I build (sandcastles / snowmen) with my father.
   나는 아빠와 모래성을 쌓는다.

 빈칸에 알맞은 단어를 단어 박스에서 찾아 넣어 이야기를 완성하세요.

Boracay Beach

Boracay _____ is in the Philippines.

The beach is famous for its lovely v_____.

Many people visit and _____ on the beach.

_____ can enjoy many things at the beach.

A woman _____ in the sun and enjoys the sunshine.

A girl wearing a bikini walks _____ the beach.

A man s_____ ice cream under a large parasol.

A _____ woman searches for shells.

A boy builds a _____.

Some kids have a _____ _____.

Little kids play in the sh_____ water.

Some people _____ the waves in the sea.

Word Box

surf   Beach   lies   sells   shallow   Visitors

fat   relax   along   views   sandcastle   water fight

Hi, Mr. Dolphin

✪ 초등 기본어휘 ◯ 중등 기본어휘 △ 확장어휘

1
✪ **sea**
명 바다
유 ocean 대양, 바다

sea

2
✪ **deep**
형 깊은

deep

3
✪ **get to**
구 도착하다
유 arrive, reach 도착하다

get to

4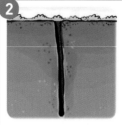
✪ **laugh**
동 웃다
명 웃음
유 giggle 낄낄 웃다

laugh

5
✪ **inside**
전 ~의 안에
반 outside ~ 밖에

inside

6
✪ **vacation**
명 방학, 휴가

vacation

7
◇ **dive**
동 잠수하다, (물속으로) 뛰어들다

dive

8
◇ **spit**
동 뱉다, 토하다

spit

9
◇ **breath**
명 숨
동 breathe 숨을 쉬다

breath

10
◇ **swallow**
동 삼키다
명 제비

swallow

11
◇ **slippery**
형 미끄러운
동 slip 미끄러지다

slippery

12
◔ **glittering**
형 반짝이는, 빛나는
유 bright 빛나는, 밝은

glittering

A 우리말 뜻에 알맞은 단어를 쓰고, 크로스워드 퍼즐을 완성하세요.

▶▶▶ ACROSS

❶ 숨 _____

❸ 방학, 휴가 _____

❺ 잠수하다 _____

❽ 미끄러운 _____

❾ 깊은 _____

▼ DOWN

❷ 삼키다 _____

❹ 웃다 _____

❻ 뱉다 _____

❼ ~의 안에 _____

❿ 바다 _____

B 연관되는 단어를 알아보고, 영어 또는 우리말 뜻을 쓰세요.

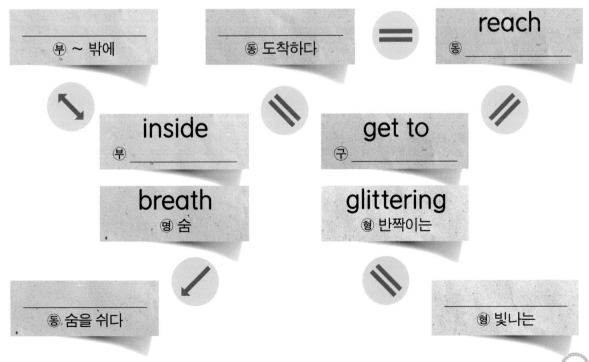

C laugh에 대해 알아보고, 빈칸에 알맞은 말을 쓰세요.

> laugh 웃다 laugh at ~을 비웃다
> ex He always laughs loudly. 그는 항상 큰소리로 웃는다.
> He laughs at me. 그는 나를 비웃는다.

1. A baby _____ on the bed. 아기가 침대에서 웃는다.

2. My sister _____ _____ my dancing. 언니가 내 춤을 비웃는다.

3. When we watch a funny movie, we _____. 재미있는 영화를 볼 때 우리는 웃는다.

4. Don't _____ _____ your friends. 친구들을 비웃지 마라.

D 문장을 읽고, 빈칸에 알맞은 단어를 쓰세요.

1. My summer _____ started yesterday. 어제 여름방학이 시작됐다.

2. I will go to the lake instead of the _____ this vacation.
   나는 이번 방학에는 바다 대신 호수에 갈 것이다.

3. The lake is really _____. 그 호수는 정말 깊다.

4. I see something _____ in the lake. It's a big goldfish.
   나는 호수에서 반짝이는 것을 본다. 그것은 큰 금붕어이다.

5. I hold my _____ and look at the goldfish. 나는 숨을 멈추고 금붕어를 본다.

6. The goldfish _____ a small fish. 금붕어가 작은 물고기를 삼킨다.

7. The goldfish sometimes _____ out water. 금붕어가 가끔 물을 내뱉는다.

8. A small fish is hiding _____ the water plants in the lake to
   avoid the goldfish. 작은 물고기가 금붕어를 피하려고 호수 안의 수풀 속으로 숨는다.

9. I try to catch the goldfish with a net. But the ground is wet and _____.
   나는 그물로 금붕어를 잡으려고 한다. 하지만 땅이 젖어서 미끄럽다.

10. All of a sudden I slip into the lake and my father _____ in to
    save me. 갑자기 내가 미끄러져 호수에 빠져서 아빠가 나를 구하기 위해 물에 뛰어든다.

 빈칸에 알맞은 단어를 단어 박스에서 찾아 넣어 이야기를 완성하세요.

Hi, Mr. Dolphin

Lucy's family goes on a summer _____ to the beach.

Her dad drives to _____ _____ the beach.

Lucy wants to explore under the s_____.

She wears goggles and _____ into the sea.

She holds her b_____ underwater.

"Look at the colorful fish. They are g_____."

She swims d_____ into the sea.

A dolphin _____ Lucy in its big mouth.

She shouts, "Ahhhhh! What happened?

It's really dark and sl_____."

She is _____ the dolphin.

She jumps up and down.

"I don't like it here."

The dolphin _____ her out.

"Oh! It's you, Mr. Dolphin!"

Mr. Dolphin _____

Word Box

| sea | laughs | slippery | dives | swallows | deeper |

| breath | vacation | glittering | spits | get to | inside |

Unit 8
I Enjoy Cooking

⭐ 초등 기본어휘 ⬦ 중등 기본어휘 ⬧ 확장어휘

1
⭐ **carrot**
ⓜ 당근

carrot

2

⭐ **potato**
ⓜ 감자

potato

3

⭐ **minute**
ⓜ 분, 순간

minute

4

⭐ **chicken**
ⓜ 닭, 닭고기

chicken

5

⭐ **how to** + 동사원형
ⓟ ~하는 방법

how to

6

⭐ **health**
ⓜ 건강
ⓗ healthy 건강한, 건강에 좋은

health

7

⬦ **fry**
ⓥ (기름에) 볶다, 튀기다

fry

8

⬦ **add**
ⓥ 더하다, 추가하다
ⓜ addition 추가, 덧셈
ⓟ subtract 빼다, 덜다

add

9

⬦ **oil**
ⓜ 기름

oil

10

⬦ **peel**
ⓥ 껍질을 벗기다
ⓜ 껍질

peel

11

⬧ **onion**
ⓜ 양파

onion

12
⬧ **ingredient**
ⓜ 재료, 원료

ingredient

A 우리말 뜻에 알맞은 단어를 쓰고, 크로스워드 퍼즐을 완성하세요.

▶▶▶ ACROSS

❶ 분, 순간 _____

❷ 기름 _____

❸ 건강 _____

❹ 감자 _____

❺ 닭, 닭고기 _____

❼ (기름에) 볶다, 튀기다 _____

▽▽ DOWN

❷ 양파 _____

❹ 껍질; 껍질을 벗기다 _____

❻ 더하다, 추가하다 _____

❽ 당근 _____

B 다음 장면에 어울리는 단어를 보기에서 골라 넣어 문장을 완성하세요.

| ingredients | potatoes | peels | how to |

1. He knows _____ make.

2. First, he prepares the _____ .

3. Second, he washes the _____ .

4. Third, he _____ the potatoes and other vegetables. Last, he cooks.

C 빈칸에 알맞은 단어를 쓰고, 사다리를 타고 내려가 정답을 확인하세요.

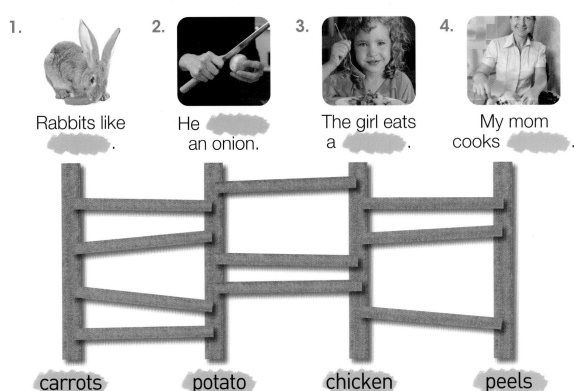

1. Rabbits like _____.

2. He _____ an onion.

3. The girl eats a _____.

4. My mom cooks _____.

carrots   potato   chicken   peels

D 문장을 읽고, 알맞은 단어에 동그라미 하세요.

1. Please prepare the (ingredients / knives) before cooking.
   요리하기 전에 재료를 준비해라.

2. Wash the chicken and (eat / peel) an onion.
   닭을 씻고 양파 껍질을 벗겨라.

3. (Fry / Chew) some chicken.   닭을 좀 튀겨라.

4. You need some (oil / fire).   기름이 좀 필요하다.

5. You have to fry it for 15 (minutes / hours).   15분 동안 그것을 튀겨야 한다.

6. Do you know (how to / what to) make the sauce?   소스 만드는 방법을 아는가?

7. (Add / Collect) some soy sauce and mix ingredients together.
   간장을 좀 더하고 재료들을 함께 섞어라.

8. And eat it with a salad. It's good for your (healthy / health).
   그리고 그것을 샐러드와 함께 먹어라. 건강에 좋다.

How to Make Chicken Curry

Curry is good for our h_____.
Let's make a delicious chicken curry for four people. Take a look.

_____:
• _____
• one _____ and
  one _____
• two _____
• 400 g _____
• curry powder
• 400~450 ml water

H_____ _____ Make:
First, _____ an onion and the other vegetables.
Second, cut up the potatoes, carrot, and onion.
Third, put them in a pan and _____ them in oil.
After that, put the chicken in and cook everything together.
Finally, _____ the curry powder and water.
Cook for 40 _____.

Word Box

Ingredients | minutes | carrot | How to | oil | peel

add | chicken | potatoes | health | onion | fry

✿ 초등 기본어휘 ◇ 중등 기본어휘 △ 확장어휘

1
✿ **egg**
몡 달걀

egg

2
✿ **hen**
몡 암탉
맨 rooster, cock 수탉

hen

3
✿ **well**
뷘 잘

well

4
✿ **happy**
혱 행복한 맨 unhappy 불행한
뷔 happier 더 행복한
쵠 happiest 가장 행복한

happy

5
✿ **tooth**
몡 이, 치아
뵥 teeth (여러 개의) 이

tooth

6
✿ **enough**
혱 충분한

enough

7
◇ **mix**
뢩 섞다, 혼합하다
뮤 combine 결합하다

mix

8
◇ **pot**
몡 냄비

pot

9
◇ **chef**
몡 주방장
뮤 cook 요리사

chef

10
Writing Contest
Topic : My Best Friend
◇ **topic**
몡 주제

topic

11
△ **simmer**
뢩 끓이다
뮤 boil 끓이다

simmer

12
△ **fridge**
몡 냉장고
뮤 refrigerator 냉장고

fridge

A 우리말 뜻에 알맞은 단어를 쓰고, 크로스워드 퍼즐을 완성하세요.

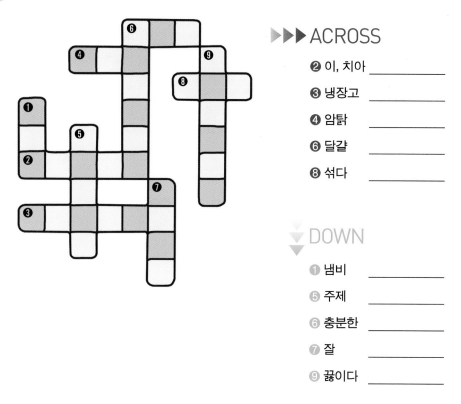

▶▶▶ ACROSS

❷ 이, 치아 _____

❸ 냉장고 _____

❹ 암탉 _____

❻ 달걀 _____

❽ 섞다 _____

▼ DOWN

❶ 냄비 _____

❺ 주제 _____

❻ 충분한 _____

❼ 잘 _____

❾ 끓이다 _____

B 연관되는 단어를 알아보고, 영어 또는 우리말 뜻을 쓰세요.

chef
명 _____

=

cook
명 _____

_____
동 끓이다

‖

_____
동 섞다

=

combine
동 _____

boil
동 _____

_____
형 행복한

→

happier
비 _____

→

_____
최 가장 행복한

C happy의 사용법에 대해 알아보고, 빈칸에 알맞은 단어를 쓰세요.

> **happy** 행복한   **happier than** ~보다 더 행복한
> ⓔⓧ I am **happy**. 나는 행복하다.   ⓔⓧ I am <u>happier than</u> you.   내가 당신보다 더 행복하다.
>
> **the happiest** 가장 행복한
> ⓔⓧ Today is <u>the happiest</u> day of my life.   오늘은 내 인생에서 가장 행복한 날이다.

1. She is _____ today.   그녀는 오늘 행복하다.

2. Poor people can be _____ than rich people.
   가난한 사람들이 부자보다 더 행복할 수도 있다.

3. She is the _____ student in our class.   그녀는 우리 반에서 가장 행복한 학생이다.

D 문장을 읽고, 빈칸에 알맞은 단어를 쓰세요.

1. My father is a _____ at a big restaurant.   아빠는 큰 식당의 주방장이다.

2. He can make salad very _____.   그는 샐러드를 아주 잘 만들 수 있다.

3. The _____ is making a healthy salad.
   주제는 건강한 샐러드 만들기이다.

4. He has _____ ingredients to make it.
   그는 그것을 만들기 위해 충분한 재료를 가지고 있다.

5. He gets a _____ from the farm.   그는 농장에서 암탉을 구한다.

6. He puts some water in a big _____.   그는 큰 냄비에 물을 좀 넣는다.

7. He _____ the chicken.   그는 닭고기를 끓인다.

8. He cuts up some boiled _____.   그는 몇 개의 삶은 달걀을 자른다.

9. He takes some fruit and vegetables out of the _____.
   그는 냉장고에서 과일과 채소들을 꺼낸다.

10. He _____ the vegetables together.   그는 채소들을 함께 섞는다.

11. He adds cheese and yogurt for healthy _____.
    그는 건강한 치아를 위해 치즈와 요거트를 더한다.

 E 빈칸에 알맞은 단어를 단어 박스에서 찾아 넣어 이야기를 완성하세요.

Giggle Gaggle* Cooking Contest

_____ : The Happiest Meal

Day: July 7

Prize: A Free Airline Ticket to France

Lucy and Mr. Cook want to join the cooking contest.

Mr. Cook is a great _____.

He cooks very _____.

They prepare some ingredients for the h_____ meal.

Lucy looks in the _____ to get some ingredients.

She takes out one _____, some potatoes, and some carrots.

Mr. Cook says, "It's not _____. We need something more."

He gets a goldfish's t_____ and some h_____'s feet.

They put them in the _____.

"Let's _____ them together," says Mr. Cook.

"Let's _____ them," says Lucy.

They finish cooking.

"Let's taste it. Wow! It's yummy. I am so happy."

"We will win the contest."

∗ **giggle gaggle** 낄낄 깔깔

Word Box

Topic · hen · simmer · chef · happiest · egg

mix · well · pot · enough · tooth · fridge

Unit 9
At the Hospital

★ 초등 기본어휘 ◇ 중등 기본어휘 △ 확장어휘

1
★ **hurt**
동 다치게 하다, 아프다

hurt

2

★ **stay**
동 머무르다

stay

3

★ **worry**
동 걱정하다

worry

4

★ **hospital**
명 병원

hospital

5

◇ **treat**
동 치료하다, 처치하다

treat

6
◇ **crowded**
형 붐비는, 복잡한
동 crowd 붐비다

crowded

7

◇ **patient**
명 환자
반 doctor 의사

patient

8

◇ **headache**
명 두통

headache

9

△ **emergency**
형 긴급한
명 위급, 비상

emergency

10

△ **bleed**
동 피가 나다
명 blood 피
형 bloody 피가 나는

bleed

11
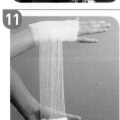
△ **bandage**
명 붕대

bandage

12
△ **symptom**
명 증상

symptom

A 우리말 뜻에 알맞은 단어를 쓰고, 크로스워드 퍼즐을 완성하세요.

▶▶▶ ACROSS

❶ 증상 _____

❸ 붕대 _____

❹ 두통 _____

❻ 피가 나다 _____

▼ DOWN

❶ 머무르다 _____

❷ 걱정하다 _____

❺ 붐비는 _____

❼ 치료하다 _____

B 다음 장면에 어울리는 단어를 보기에서 골라 넣어 문장을 완성하세요.

| patient | treats | emergency | hospital |

1. A _____ is taken out of the ambulance.

2. Doctors are waiting at the _____ .

3. The patient is carried to the _____ room.

4. A doctor _____ the patient.

C 빈칸에 알맞은 단어를 쓰고, 사다리를 타고 내려가 정답을 확인하세요.

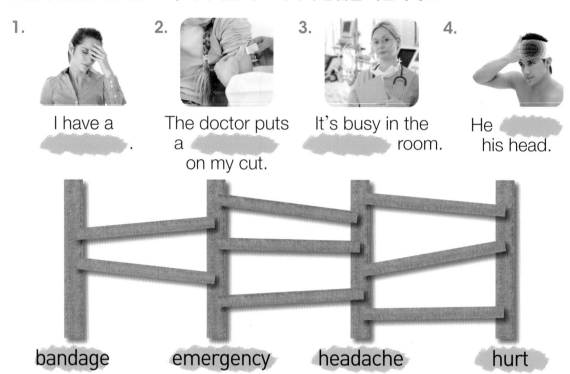

1. I have a _____ .

2. The doctor puts a _____ on my cut.

3. It's busy in the _____ room.

4. He _____ his head.

bandage   emergency   headache   hurt

D 문장을 읽고, 알맞은 단어에 동그라미 하세요.

1. My mother is in the (post office / hospital) now. 엄마는 지금 병원에 있다.

2. It is (crowded / crown). 그곳은 붐빈다.

3. My mom is a (patient / doctor). 우리 엄마는 환자이다.

4. The doctor says my mom's (system / symptoms) will get better.
   의사는 엄마의 증상들이 점점 나아질 거라고 말한다.

5. She (bleeds / bloods) a lot after her surgery. 그녀는 수술 후에 피를 많이 흘린다.

6. I'll (move / stay) at the hospital to take care of my mom tonight.
   나는 오늘 밤 엄마를 돌보기 위해서 병원에 머물 것이다.

7. I will try not to (berry / worry) about my mom.
   나는 엄마를 걱정하지 않으려고 노력할 것이다.

8. The doctor will (treat / trade) the symptoms with medicine.
   의사는 그 증상들을 약으로 치료할 것이다.

 빈칸에 알맞은 단어를 단어 박스에서 찾아 넣어 이야기를 완성하세요.

In the Emergency Room

Sick people go to the _____.

The _____ room (ER) is busy all day.

It is open 24 hours a day.

It is the most _____ place in the hospital.

A boy who has a h_____ is crying.

His mother _____ about him.

A b_____ man is carried in on a stretcher* from the ambulance.

He _____ his arm. A nurse puts a _____ on his arm.

Doctors and nurses s_____ there all day.

They are always busy taking care of _____.

Sick people have various sy_____.

Doctors and nurses _____ them in different ways.

Lots of lives are saved in the ER.

*stretcher 들것

Word Box

worries	symptoms	emergency	hospital	hurt	stay
patients	bleeding	bandage	crowded	headache	treat

Lucy Becomes a Doctor

✪ 초등 기본어휘   ◇ 중등 기본어휘   △ 확장어휘

1

✪ **ill**
형 아픈
유 sick 아픈
명 illness 아픔

ill

2

こんにちは
✪ **be able to**
구 ~할 수 있다
유 can ~할 수 있다

be able to

3

✪ **excellent**
형 훌륭한
유 great 훌륭한, 대단한

excellent

4

✪ **take a rest**
구 쉬다
유 take a break 쉬다

take a rest

5

✪ **fall in love**
구 사랑에 빠지다

fall in love

6

✪ **stomachache**
명 복통

stomachache

7

I'm scared.
◇ **pretend**
동 ~인 체하다

pretend

8

◇ **instead of**
구 ~ 대신에

instead of

9
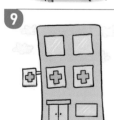
△ **clinic**
명 개인병원

clinic

10

△ **disguise**
동 변장시키다, 속이다

disguise

11

△ **give a shot**
구 주사를 놓다

give a shot

12

△ **prescribe**
동 처방하다
명 prescription 처방전

prescribe

A 우리말 뜻에 알맞은 단어를 쓰고, 크로스워드 퍼즐을 완성하세요.

▶▶▶ ACROSS

❶ 주사를 놓다 _____

❹ 개인병원 _____

❺ 휴식을 취하다 _____

❼ 변장시키다 _____

▼ DOWN

❷ 복통 _____

❸ 사랑에 빠지다 _____

❻ ~인 체하다 _____

❽ ~ 대신에 _____

B 연관되는 단어를 알아보고, 영어 또는 우리말 뜻을 쓰세요.

illness
명 아픔
← ill
형 _____
= sick
형 _____

excellent
형 _____
= _____
형 훌륭한

be able to
구 _____

prescription
명 _____
← prescribe
동 _____

_____
동 ~할 수 있다

C 신체 부위 뒤에 -ache를 붙여서 통증을 나타내요. 빈칸에 알맞은 단어를 쓰세요.

head 머리 + ache 아픔 ○ headache 두통
stomach 위, 배 + ache 아픔 ○ stomachache 복통
back 허리 + ache 아픔 ○ backache 요통
tooth 치아 + ache 아픔 ○ toothache 치통

1. If you eat too much, you'll get a _____. 과식하면, 배가 아플 것이다.

2. He has a _____. 그는 두통이 있다.

3. I think a _____ is the most painful. 나는 치통이 가장 고통스럽다고 생각한다.

D 문장을 읽고, 빈칸에 알맞은 말을 쓰세요.

1. Sophia is an _____ doctor. 소피아는 훌륭한 의사이다.

2. Her _____ is always open. 그녀의 개인병원은 항상 문을 연다.

3. Sophia has been _____ for the past few days.
소피아는 지난 며칠 동안 아팠다.

4. She _____ that she's fine. 그녀는 괜찮은 척한다.

5. She says, "I'll _____ _____ _____ go to work."
"나는 일하러 갈 수 있을 거야."라고 그녀가 말한다.

6. A magician _____ _____ _____ with her.
한 마법사가 그녀와 사랑에 빠진다.

7. He _____ himself as a doctor. 그는 의사로 변장한다.

8. He says, "You need to _____ _____ _____."
"당신은 휴식이 필요해요."라고 그가 말한다.

9. "_____ _____ working, just lie down." "일하는 대신 그냥 누워 있어요."

10. He _____ her some medicine. 그가 그녀에게 약을 처방해 준다.

11. The nurse _____ her _____ _____ in her arm.
간호사가 그녀의 팔에 주사를 놓는다.

빈칸에 알맞은 단어를 단어 박스에서 찾아 넣어 이야기를 완성하세요.

Lucy Becomes a Doctor

Lucy's father is a doctor.

One day, he got sick and wasn't _____ to go to work.

Lucy decided to go to work i_____ _____ her father.

She _____ herself as a doctor.

When she wore a white coat, she looked like her father.

A boy came to the _____ with his mother.

He p_____ to be _____ because he didn't want to go to school.

"I have a _____," said the boy.

Lucy _____ the boy some fake medicine.

The next patient was a man who _____ _____ _____.

Lucy told him to stand on his head for 5 minutes.

She thought it would stop him for thinking about her.

A woman who felt blue* came to Lucy.

Lucy _____ her _____ _____,

which made her feel better.

Lucy also told her to _____ _____ _____.

She did an _____ job as a doctor.

*feel blue 기분이 우울하다

Word Box

prescribed   able   stomachache   fell in love   disguised   take a rest

pretended   clinic   instead of   ill   gave ~ a shot   excellent

Unit 10
Roller Coaster

Why Do People Like Roller Coasters?

⭐ 초등 기본어휘 ◇ 중등 기본어휘 ⌂ 확장어휘

1
⭐ **top**
- 명 꼭대기
- 유 peak 산꼭대기, 최고조

top

2
⭐ **guess**
- 동 추측하다
- 명 추측

guess

3
⭐ **rider**
- 명 타는 사람
- 동명 ride 타다; 탈것

rider

4
⭐ **which**
- 대 어느 것
- 형 어느

which

5
⭐ **because**
- 접 ~ 때문에

because

6
◇ **fear**
- 명 공포
- 동 무서워하다
- 유 horror 공포

fear

7
◇ **while**
- 접 ~하는 동안

while

8
◇ **located**
- 형 ~에 위치한
- 동 locate 위치하다

located

9
◇ **increase**
- 동 증가하다
- 반 decrease 감소하다

increase

10
◇ **rapidly**
- 부 빠르게, 급격하게
- 형 rapid 빠른

rapidly

11
⌂ **thrill**
- 명 전율, 흥분, 설렘
- 동 열광시키다, 감동시키다
- 형 thrilled 흥분한

thrill

12
⌂ **at the same time**
- 구 동시에, 잠깐, 잠시
- 유 at the same moment 동시에

at the same time

A 우리말 뜻에 알맞은 단어를 쓰고, 크로스워드 퍼즐을 완성하세요.

▶▶▶ACROSS

❶ 어느 것 _____

❷ ~하는 동안 _____

❹ 급격하게 _____

❻ ~ 때문에 _____

❽ 추측하다 _____

❾ 타는 사람 _____

▼ DOWN

❸ 전율 _____

❺ 증가하다 _____

❼ 공포 _____

❿ ~에 위치한 _____

B 다음 장면에 어울리는 단어를 보기에서 골라 넣어 문장을 완성하세요.

| thrill | top | fear | at the same time |

1. I like bungee jumping off the _____ of the mountain.

2. I feel different feelings _____.

3. I get a _____ and feel _____. Why don't you try it?

C 빈칸에 알맞은 단어를 쓰고, 사다리를 타고 내려가 정답을 확인하세요.

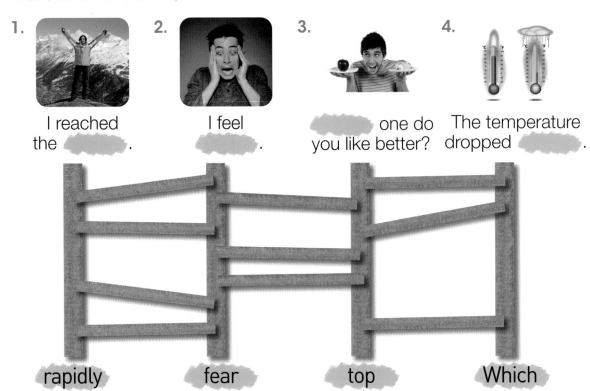

1. I reached the _____.

2. I feel _____.

3. _____ one do you like better?

4. The temperature dropped _____.

rapidly   fear   top   Which

D 문장을 읽고, 알맞은 단어에 동그라미 하세요.

1. Disneyland is (located / pushed) in California. 디즈니랜드는 캘리포니아에 위치해 있다.

2. I'm (boring / thrilled) about going to Disneyland.
   나는 디즈니랜드에 가는 것에 흥분된다.

3. The ticket price has (increased / breaks) a lot. 표 가격이 많이 올랐다.

4. (Understand / Guess) how much the ticket is. 표가 얼마일지 맞춰 봐라.

5. I love it (because / which) I can enjoy exciting rides.
   나는 신나는 놀이 기구들을 즐길 수 있기 때문에 디즈니랜드를 아주 좋아한다.

6. I feel happy (why / while) riding the merry-go-round.
   나는 회전목마를 타는 동안 행복하다.

7. The (riders / readers) wait for their turn. 타는 사람들이 자신들의 순서를 기다린다.

8. Parents and kids can all be happy (at the same time / at the moment)
   in Disneyland. 디즈니랜드에서는 부모님과 아이들이 동시에 모두 행복해질 수 있다.

 E 빈칸에 알맞은 단어를 단어 박스에서 찾아 넣어 이야기를 완성하세요.

Why Do People Like Roller Coasters?

People like to ride roller coasters.

Can you _____ the reason?

It's _____ the speed makes people excited.

Roller coasters go slowly to the t_____.

The r_____ feel excited and nervous

w_____ it's going up to the top.

The roller coaster w_____ reaches

the top goes down ra_____.

The speed of the roller coaster _____.

A sudden change in speed makes people get

a t_____.

Also they feel _____.

They experience two feelings _____

_____ _____ _____.

What is the fastest roller coaster in the world?

It's Formula Rossa, _____ at Ferrari

World in the United Arab Emirates.

People from all over the world go there to ride it.

Word Box

at the same time	thrill	top	fear	guess	because

riders	rapidly	increases	while	located	which

An Adventure with a Genie

☆ 초등 기본어휘 ◇ 중등 기본어휘 △ 확장어휘

1
☆ **buy**
통 사다
반 sell 팔다
과 bought 샀다

buy

2
☆ **gate**
명 출입문, 대문

gate

3
☆ **seat**
명 좌석, 자리

seat

4
☆ **thirsty**
형 목마른

thirsty

5
☆ **yesterday**
명 어제
명 today 오늘
명 tomorrow 내일

yesterday

6
◇ **lamp**
명 등불, 램프

lamp

7
◇ **steal**
통 훔치다

steal

8
◇ **escape**
통 탈출하다
명 탈출

escape

9
◇ **moment**
명 순간

moment

10
◇ **imagine**
통 상상하다
명 imagination 상상, 상상력

imagine

11
◇ **adventure**
명 모험
형 adventurous 모험심이 강한

adventure

12
△ **maze**
명 미로

maze

A 우리말 뜻에 알맞은 단어를 쓰고, 크로스워드 퍼즐을 완성하세요.

▶▶▶ ACROSS

❶ 모험 _____
❸ 순간 _____
❺ 좌석, 자리 _____
❻ 사다 _____
❽ 등불, 램프 _____

▼ DOWN

❷ 훔치다 _____
❸ 미로 _____
❹ 목이 마른 _____
❼ 출입문, 대문 _____
❾ 탈출하다 _____

B 연관되는 단어를 알아보고, 영어 또는 우리말 뜻을 쓰세요.

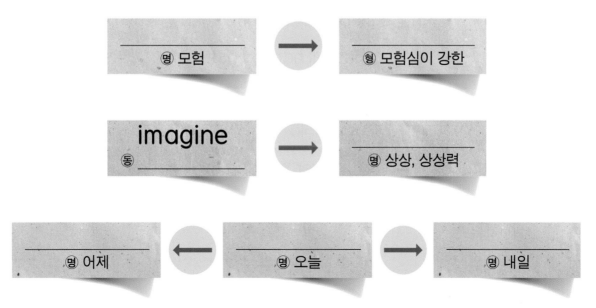

_____ (명) 모험 ➡ _____ (형) 모험심이 강한

imagine (동) _____ ➡ _____ (명) 상상, 상상력

_____ (명) 어제 ⬅ _____ (명) 오늘 ➡ _____ (명) 내일

C seat가 들어간 다양한 표현을 알아보고, 빈칸에 알맞은 말을 쓰세요.

> seatbelt 안전 벨트   a window seat 창가 자리
> an aisle seat 통로 자리

1. Fasten your _____. 안전 벨트를 매라.

2. I would like a _____ _____. 나는 창가 자리를 원한다.

3. He would like an _____ _____. 그는 통로 자리를 원한다.

D 문장을 읽고, 빈칸에 알맞은 단어를 쓰세요.

1. The genie lives in a _____. 지니는 램프 안에 산다.

2. He likes to read _____ stories. 그는 모험 이야기들을 읽는 것을 좋아한다.

3. _____ was his birthday. 어제는 그의 생일이었다.

4. I _____ a storybook for him. 나는 그를 위해 이야기 책을 샀다.

5. He _____ what will happen at the end. 그는 끝에 무슨 일이 일어날지 상상한다.

6. He sees a _____ in the story. 이야기 속에서 그는 미로를 본다.

7. He _____ some gold from the maze. 그는 미로에서 금을 조금 훔친다.

8. He gets _____ after running through the maze. 미로 속을 달린 후에 그는 목이 마르다.

9. He finds a _____ behind him. 그는 뒤에 있는 문을 발견한다.

10. He _____ from the maze. 그는 미로를 탈출한다.

11. At that _____, he shouts for joy. 그 순간, 그는 기뻐서 소리친다.

E 빈칸에 알맞은 단어를 단어 박스에서 찾아 넣어 이야기를 완성하세요.

An Adventure with a Genie

Lucy went to the amusement park _____.

Lucy felt _____.

So Lucy _____ a bottle of water and drank it.

"You can get what you _____ if you drink this," was written on the bottle. Lucy rode on the roller coaster.

Lucy thought about Aladdin's magic _____.

Then, a magic lamp and a genie appeared in Lucy's hand.

And a wizard appeared in the back s_____.

He tried to st_____ the lamp.

Lucy and the genie went into the m_____.

But Lucy wanted to _____ from the maze.

"Find the _____, please, Genie," said Lucy.

At that _____, Lucy appeared on the outside of the gate.

The genie said, "Goodbye. It's time to go home."

Lucy went home and told her family about her _____ with the genie.

Word Box

| gate | maze | escape | moment | bought | lamp |

| adventure | yesterday | steal | thirsty | imagine | seat |

Unit 1
My Collection
나의 수집

• Lesson 1 • **Collecting Bills and Coins** p.10

Ⓐ

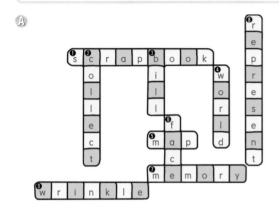

▶▶ ACROSS

❶ scrapbook ❺ map ❼ memory ❾ wrinkle

▾ DOWN

❷ collect ❸ bill ❹ world ❻ face
❽ represent

Ⓑ 1. money 2. coins 3. bills 4. When

Ⓒ 1. map 2. coin 3. memory 4. money

Ⓓ 1. world 2. when 3. bills 4. collected
5. scrapbook 6. wrinkle 7. faces 8. represent

Ⓔ **Collecting Bills and Coins** p.13

This is my money collection.
I collect money when I travel all over the world.
I collect money to remember my trips.

My coins are on my world map. The coins look different.
There are great people's faces on the coins.
Things that represent each country are on the coins, too.
I tape coins to my world map.

Bills are made of a special kind of paper.
There are pictures of important people and places on the bills, too.
I put them in a scrapbook, so they will not get wrinkled.
Whenever I see my collection, I think about my memories

from my trips. That makes me happy.

● 해석 ●
지폐와 동전 수집하기
이것은 나의 돈 수집품이다.
나는 전세계를 여행할 때 돈을 수집한다.
나는 나의 여행을 기억하기 위해 돈을 수집한다.

내 동전들이 세계지도 위에 있다. 동전들이 달라 보인다.
동전에 위인들의 얼굴이 있다.
각 나라를 대표하는 것들도 동전에 있다.
나는 동전들을 내 세계지도 위에 테이프로 붙인다.

지폐는 특수한 종이로 만든다.
중요한 인물과 장소들의 그림도 지폐에 그려져 있다.
나는 지폐들을 스크랩북에 넣는다. 그래서 구겨지지 않을 것이다.
내 수집품을 볼 때마다 여행의 추억들을 생각한다. 그것은 나를 행복하게 한다.

• Lesson 2 • **Lucy's Nap with Her Dolls** p.14

Ⓐ

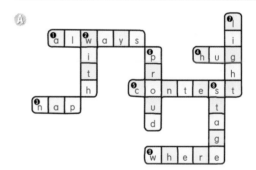

▶▶ ACROSS

❶ always ❸ nap ❹ hug ❺ contest
❾ where

▾ DOWN

❷ with ❻ proud ❼ light ❽ stage

Ⓑ

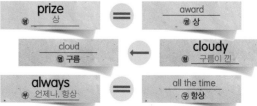

ⓒ 1. alive   2. asleep   3. sleep   4. live

ⓓ 1. with   2. stage   3. Where   4. always

   5. naps   6. contest   7. lights   8. prize

   9. hugs   10. proud

ⓔ Lucy's Nap with Her Dolls   p.17

Lucy's hobby is collecting Blythe dolls.

She likes playing <u>with</u> her dolls.

She a<u>lways</u> brings them with her.

One day, she takes a <u>nap</u> on the sofa.

She is h<u>ugging</u> her doll.

It's so c<u>loudy</u> in her dream.

Suddenly, there is a <u>light</u>, but she can't open her eyes.

She can't believe <u>where</u> she is.

It's a Blythe doll modeling <u>contest</u>.

All the dolls are <u>alive</u> and look wonderful.

Her favorite Blythe doll is on the <u>stage</u>.

She has long blond hair and beautiful green eyes.

She wins the first <u>prize</u> and wears the crown.

She is the most beautiful Blythe doll in the world.

Lucy is so <u>proud</u> of her.

When Lucy wakes up from the dream, she finds the doll.

● 해석 ●

인형과 함께 한 루시의 낮잠

루시의 취미는 블라이스 인형들을 수집하는 것이다.

그녀는 그녀의 인형들과 노는 것을 좋아한다.

그녀는 언제나 그것들을 가지고 다닌다.

어느 날, 그녀는 소파에서 낮잠을 잔다.

그녀는 그녀의 인형을 안고 있다.

그녀의 꿈 속에는 구름이 잔뜩 끼어있다.

갑자기 빛이 나고, 그녀는 눈을 뜰 수가 없다.

그녀는 그녀가 어디에 있는 지 믿을 수가 없다.

이곳은 블라이스 인형 모델 대회이다.

모든 인형들이 살아 있고 멋있어 보인다.

그녀가 가장 좋아하는 블라이스 인형이 무대 위에 있다.

그녀는 긴 금발머리와 초록색 눈을 갖고 있다.

그녀는 1등을 해서 왕관을 쓴다.

그녀는 세상에서 가장 아름다운 블라이스 인형이다.

루시는 그녀가 정말 자랑스럽다.

꿈에서 깨어나자 루시는 그 인형을 발견한다.

Unit 2 — Amazing B-Boy Dancers
놀라운 비보이 댄서들

• Lesson 1 • Korean B-Boy Teams   p.18

ⓐ
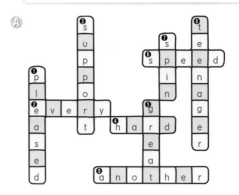

▶▶▶ ACROSS

❷ every   ❹ hard   ❻ speed   ❾ another

▽ DOWN

❶ pleased   ❸ support   ❺ great   ❼ spin

❽ teenager

ⓑ 1. dances   2. teenager   3. amazing

   4. spins, speeds

ⓒ 1. another   2. hard   3. pleased   4. speed

ⓓ 1. teenager   2. dance   3. spins   4. Every

   5. great   6. amazing   7. support

   8. give them a big hand

ⓔ Korean B-Boy Teams   p.21

Do you like B-boy <u>dances</u>?

B-boy dances are popular among t<u>eenagers</u>.

Look at the B-boy dancers!

They are really a<u>mazing</u>.

One B-boy dancer s<u>pins</u> at high <u>speeds</u>.

<u>Another</u> B-boy dancer su<u>pports</u> his body with only one arm.

Their dance is perfect.

People watch them dance and g<u>ive</u> them <u>a big hand</u>.

They practice really h<u>ard</u>.

Practice makes them perfect.

<u>Every</u> year, the U.K. Championship is held.

The Korean B-boy teams took part in the U.K. Championship.
They were so <u>great</u> that they won many prizes.
Many fans were <u>pleased</u> to hear about their success.

● 해석 ●

한국의 비보이 팀들
여러분은 비보이 춤을 좋아하는가?
비보이 춤은 십대들 사이에서 인기가 있다.

저 비보이 댄서들을 보라!
그들은 정말 놀랍다.
한 비보이 댄서가 빠른 속도로 돌고 있다.
다른 비보이 댄서는 오직 한 팔로 몸을 지탱한다.
그들의 춤은 완벽하다.

사람들은 그들이 춤추는 것을 보고 큰 박수를 보내고 있다.
그들은 정말 열심히 연습한다.
연습은 그들을 완벽하게 해준다.

매년, 영국 챔피언십이 열린다.
한국의 비보이 팀들도 영국 챔피언십에 참가했다.
그들은 정말 대단해서 많은 상을 탔다.
많은 팬들은 그들의 성공 소식을 듣고서 기뻐했다.

• Lesson 2 • **A B-Boy Prince** p.22

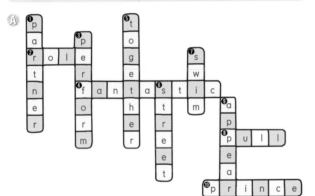

▶▶ ACROSS

❷ role ❹ fantastic ❽ pull ❿ prince

▾ DOWN

❶ partner ❸ perform ❺ together ❻ street
❼ swim ❾ appear

Ⓑ
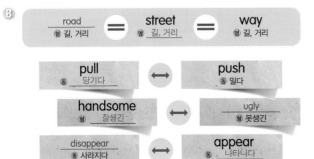

Ⓒ 1. swimming   2. Shopping   3. running

Ⓓ 1. performed   2. street   3. prince
4. went down, his knees   5. roles   6. handsome
7. together   8. pulled   9. fantastic   10. appeared

Ⓔ **A B-Boy Prince** p.25

Lucy practices ballet at a ballet academy.
She is going to <u>perform</u> Swan Lake.
She takes the <u>role</u> of Odette.
But she has no dance par<u>tner</u> yet.
One day, Lucy sees a <u>street</u> dance performance.
The B-boy dancers dance really well.
It is amazing to watch their dance.
A h<u>andsome</u> B-boy dancer grabs Lucy's hand.
He <u>pulls</u> her up on stage.
Lucy dances on the stage with him.
Suddenly, she falls into a f<u>antastic</u> world.
The B-boy dancer changes into a <u>prince</u> and swims in
the lake.
Lucy becomes a swan and sw<u>ims</u> in the lake, too.
Suddenly, the handsome B-boy prince a<u>ppears</u>.
He <u>goes</u> <u>down</u> on one knee and proposes to her.
Then, Lucy becomes a beautiful princess.
They dance <u>together</u> under the moonlight.

● 해석 ●

비보이 왕자
루시는 발레 학원에서 발레를 연습한다.
그녀는 '백조의 호수'를 공연할 것이다.
그녀는 오데뜨 역할을 맡는다.
그러나 그녀는 아직 댄스 파트너가 없다.
어느 날, 루시는 길거리 댄스 공연을 본다.
그 비보이 댄서들은 춤을 매우 잘 춘다.
그들의 춤을 보는 것은 놀랍다.
잘생긴 비보이 댄서가 루시의 손을 잡는다.
그는 그녀를 무대 위로 잡아당긴다.
루시는 무대 위에서 그와 함께 춤을 춘다.
갑자기, 그녀는 환상적인 세계로 떨어진다.
비보이 댄서가 왕자로 변해 호수에서 수영을 한다.
루시도 백조가 되어 호수에서 수영을 한다.
갑자기, 잘생긴 비보이 왕자가 나타난다.
그는 한쪽 무릎을 꿇고 그녀에게 프로포즈를 한다.
그러자, 루시는 아름다운 공주가 된다.
그들은 달빛 아래서 함께 춤을 춘다.

Unit 3

Murphy's Law
머피의 법칙

• Lesson 1 • **The Meaning of Murphy's Law** p.26

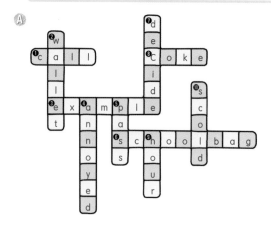

▶▶ ACROSS

❶ call　　　❸ example　　　❻ school bag　❽ Coke

DOWN

❷ wallet　　❹ annoyed　　　❺ pass　　　❼ decide
❾ hour　　　❿ scold

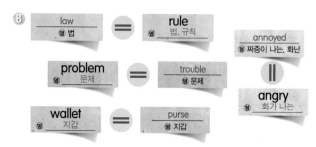

Ⓒ 1. Coke　　2. school bag　　3. decided　　4. laws

Ⓓ 1. example　2. problem　　3. wallet　　4. passed
　 5. called　 6. hour　　　 7. scolded　 8. annoyed

Ⓔ **The Meaning of Murphy's Law**　p.29

Do you know Murphy's <u>Law</u>?
When anything that can go wrong does go wrong,
we <u>call</u> this Murphy's Law.
Let me give you some <u>examples</u>.
　– You wait for the bus for an <u>hour</u>, but it doesn't arrive.
You <u>decide</u> to take a taxi.

But as soon as you get in it, the bus <u>passes</u> by.
This is Murphy's Law.
　– You lose your <u>wallet</u> and buy a new one.
Then you find it in your <u>school bag</u>.
This is Murphy's Law.
　– Your mom <u>scolds</u> you for something you didn't do, so
you are a<u>nnoyed</u>.
You kick a can of <u>Coke</u>.
It hits a police officer's head and you have some
<u>problems</u>.
This is Murphy's Law.

● 해석 ●
머피의 법칙의 의미
너는 머피의 법칙에 대해 알고 있니?
잘못될 수 있는 어떤 일이 잘못되면 우리는 이것을 머피의 법칙이라고
부른다.
몇 가지 예를 들어보자.
- 한 시간 동안 버스를 기다리는데 버스가 오지 않는다.
너는 택시를 타기로 결정한다.
그런데 네가 택시를 타자마자 버스가 지나간다.
이것이 머피의 법칙이다.
- 지갑을 잃어버려서 새 것을 산다.
그런데 그것을 책가방 속에서 찾는다.
이것이 머피의 법칙이다.
- 엄마가 네가 하지 않은 일로 꾸중하신다.
그래서 너는 짜증이 난다.
너는 콜라 캔을 찬다.
그것이 경찰관의 머리에 맞아서 곤란한 처지가 된다.
이것이 머피의 법칙이다.

• Lesson 2 • **An Unlucky Day**　p.30

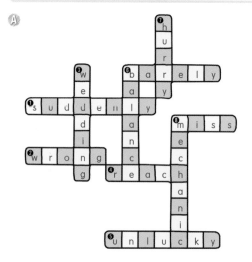

Unit 4

Mom's Words
엄마의 말들

▶▶ ACROSS

❶ suddenly ❷ wrong ❹ reach ❺ unlucky

❻ barely ❽ miss

DOWN

❸ wedding ❻ balance ❼ hurry ❽ mechanic

Ⓑ 1. office 2. balance 3. fell on his face

4. unlucky

Ⓒ 1. sudden 2. suddenly 3. unlucky 4. Unluckily

Ⓓ 1. mechanic 2. office 3. wedding 4. hurries

5. misses 6. wrong 7. balance

8. falls, his face 9. barely 10. reaches

Ⓔ **An Unlucky Day** p.33

Lucy's aunt has a wedding today.

Lucy's father doesn't go to the office.

Lucy and her family go to the wedding.

Lucy's father starts the engine but it doesn't work.

"What's wrong with the car? We should call a mechanic."

When the mechanic arrives, the car starts by itself.

Vroom, vroom. Her father rushes to the wedding.

"Hurry up, or we will miss the wedding!"

Suddenly, a car hits Lucy's car.

"Ahhhh! We will be late for the wedding!"

They reach the wedding just in time.

"We barely made it. Come on. Run, run!"

Lucy steps on her long dress and loses her balance.

She falls flat on her face.

"Oh, my god! What an unlucky day!"

● 해석 ●

운이 나쁜 날

오늘은 루시의 고모의 결혼식이다.

루시의 아빠는 사무실에 가지 않는다.

루시와 가족들은 결혼식에 간다.

루시의 아빠가 시동을 걸지만 시동이 걸리지 않는다.

"차에 무슨 문제가 있는 거지? 자동차 정비공을 불러야겠다."

정비공이 도착하자 차는 저절로 시동이 걸린다.

부릉, 부릉. 루시 아빠는 서둘러 결혼식에 간다.

"서둘러, 그렇지 않으면 우리는 결혼식을 놓칠 거야!"

갑자기 어떤 차가 루시의 차를 친다.

"아! 결혼식에 늦겠다!"

그들은 결혼식에 가까스로 때 맞추어 도착한다.

"우리는 간신히 도착했어. 어서 가자. 달려, 달려!"

루시는 그녀의 긴 드레스를 밟고 균형을 잃는다.

그녀는 앞으로 납작하게 넘어진다.

"오, 이런! 정말 운이 나쁜 날이다!"

• Lesson 1 • **To My Lovely Daughter** p.34

Ⓐ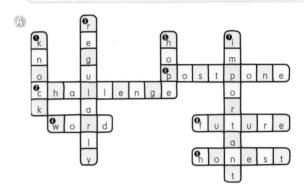

▶▶ ACROSS

❷ challenge ❹ word ❻ postpone ❽ future

❾ honest

DOWN

❶ knock ❸ regularly ❺ hope ❼ important

Ⓑ 1. various 2. healthy 3. regularly 4. important

Ⓒ 1. various 2. knock 3. regularly 4. healthy

Ⓓ 1. future 2. come true 3. hope 4. challenge

5. words 6. important 7. postpone 8. honest

Ⓔ **To My Lovely Daughter** p.37

My daughter, Lily.

I love you very much.

So I'll tell you something important.

Please listen to my words.

I want you to have big dreams for your future.

I really want your dreams to come true.

And I want you to be healthy.

I want you to exercise regularly.

I want you to read various books.

I want you to challenge yourself.

Do what you have never done before.

And be honest. Don't tell lies.

Knock on the door before you enter another person's room.

I really hope that you live a happy life.

Oh, one more thing.

Please don't <u>postpone</u> what you have to do.
From Mom

● 해석 ●

나의 사랑하는 딸에게
나의 딸 릴리야.
나는 너를 정말 사랑한단다.
그래서 내가 너에게 중요한 몇 가지를 말할게.
제발 내 말을 들어라.
나는 네가 너의 미래를 위해 큰 꿈을 가지기를 바란다.
나는 정말 네 꿈이 이루어지기를 바란다.
그리고 나는 네가 건강하기를 바란다.
나는 네가 규칙적으로 운동하기를 바란다.
나는 네가 다양한 책들을 읽기를 바란다.
나는 네가 스스로 도전하기를 바란다.
네가 예전에 한번도 해보지 않은 것을 해보렴.
그리고 정직해라. 거짓말 하지 말아라.
다른 사람의 방에 들어가기 전엔 문을 노크하렴.
나는 정말로 네가 행복하게 살기를 바란다.
아, 한 가지 더.
제발 네가 해야할 일을 뒤로 미루지 말아라.
엄마로부터

• Lesson 2 • **Mom's Nagging** p.38

Ⓐ
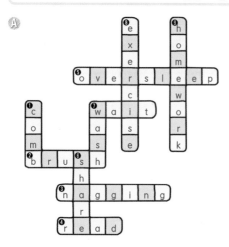

▶▶▶ ACROSS

❷ brush ❸ nagging ❹ read ❺ oversleep
❼ wait

⬇ DOWN

❶ comb ❻ share ❼ wash ❽ exercise
❾ homework

Ⓑ
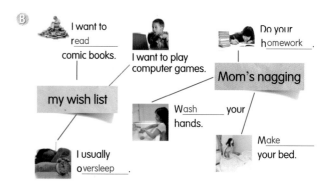

I want to
r<u>ea</u>d
comic books.

I want to play
computer games.

Do your
h<u>o</u>mework .

Mom's nagging

my wish list

W<u>a</u>sh your
hands.

I usually
o<u>ve</u>rsleep .

M<u>a</u>ke
your bed.

Ⓒ 1. wait 2. to 3. waits for

Ⓓ 1. oversleep 2. Make, bed 3. wash 4. homework
5. share 6. brushes 7. combs 8. nagging
9. chew 10. reads 11. Exercise

Ⓔ **Mom's Nagging** p.41

Today is Sunday. Lucy is sleeping.
Lucy's mom is <u>nagging</u> Lucy.
"Don't o<u>ver</u>sleep."
"<u>Wash</u> your face."
"<u>Brush</u> your teeth."
"<u>Comb</u> your hair."
"<u>Make</u> your <u>bed</u>."
"Don't eat too much fast food. Ch<u>ew</u> slowly. "
"<u>Exercise</u> every day to be healthy."
"<u>Read</u> many books."
"<u>Share</u> your things with your friends."
"W<u>ait</u> your turn."
"Do your <u>homework</u>."
"What are you going to do first?"
Lucy says, "Ah~ I'm tired of my mom's nagging.
I want to live in a world where there's no nagging."

● 해석 ●

엄마의 잔소리
오늘은 일요일이다. 루시는 잠을 자고 있다.
루시의 엄마가 루시에게 잔소리를 하고 있다.
"늦잠 자지 말아라."
"세수해라."
"양치질해라."
"머리 빗어라."
"잠자리를 정돈해라."
"패스트푸드를 너무 많이 먹지 말아라. 천천히 씹어라."
"건강해지기 위해 매일 운동해라."
"많은 책을 읽어라."
"네 물건들을 친구들과 함께 써라."
"네 순서를 기다려라."
"숙제해라."

"너 뭐 먼저 할거니?"
루시가 말한다. "아~ 엄마 잔소리가 지겨워.
난 잔소리가 없는 세상에서 살고 싶어."

Unit 5
Bookworm
책벌레

• Lesson 1 • **Children's Book Awards** p.42

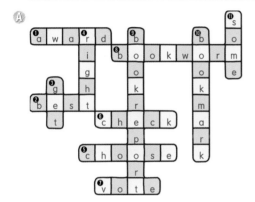

▶▶▶ ACROSS

❶ award   ❷ best   ❺ choose   ❻ check

❼ vote   ❽ bookworm

▽ DOWN

❸ get   ❹ right   ❾ book report   ❿ bookmark

⓫ some

Ⓑ 1. bookworm   2. some   3. fiction   4. book report

Ⓒ 1. bookmark   2. award   3. bookworm   4. fiction

Ⓓ 1. best   2. vote   3. choose   4. book reports
   5. checks   6. some   7. gets   8. right

Ⓔ **Children's Book Awards**   p.45

It's time for the Children's Book <u>Awards</u>.
Go to the school library and <u>choose</u> the book you like
the b<u>est</u>.
What's your favorite book?
<u>Check</u> your favorite book.
V<u>ote</u> for the best book.
   • <u>Fiction</u>

- *James and the Giant Peach, Charlotte's Web, Harry Potter*
   • Nonfiction
- *The Diary of Anne Frank, The Great Invention, The Seven Habits of Happy Kids*

There are also <u>some</u> wonderful activities.
You can meet writers and <u>get</u> autographs.
You can make your own b<u>ookmark</u>.
You can share your <u>book report</u> with your friends.
Then we'll give a prize to the <u>bookworm</u> who reads over
10 books a month.
Please come <u>right</u> away!

● 해석 ●
어린이 도서 시상식
어린이 도서 시상식 시간이 왔어요.
학교 도서관에 가서 여러분이 가장 좋아하는 책을 고르세요.
여러분이 가장 좋아하는 책은 무엇인가요?
여러분이 가장 좋아하는 책을 확인하세요.
최고의 책에 투표를 하세요.
   • 픽션(허구)
제임스와 거대한 복숭아, 샬롯의 거미줄, 해리포터
   • 논픽션(비허구)
안네 프랑크의 일기, 위대한 발명품, 행복한 아이들의 7가지 습관
또한 몇 가지 멋진 활동들이 있어요.
여러분은 작가들을 만나고 사인을 받을 수 있어요.
여러분은 여러분만의 책갈피를 만들 수 있어요.
여러분은 친구들과 함께 독후감을 나눌 수 있어요.
그리고 나서 우리는 한 달에 10권 이상을 읽은 책벌레에게 상을 수여할
거예요.
지금 바로 오세요!

• Lesson 2 • **A Gift from Harry**   p.46

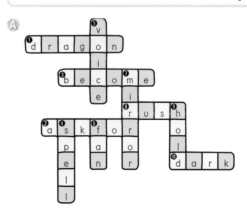

▶▶▶ ACROSS

❶ dragon   ❷ ask for   ❸ become   ❽ rush

❿ dark

▼ DOWN

④ spell   ⑤ voice   ⑥ fan   ⑦ mirror

⑨ hold

Ⓑ

brave	형 용감한	=	courageous	형 용감한
dark	명 어둠	↔	light	명 빛
wizard	명 마법사	=	witch	명 마녀

| hold | 동 잡다 |
| = |
| grasp | 동 붙잡다 |

Ⓒ 1. asks   2. asks   3. ask for   4. asks, for

Ⓓ 1. brave   2. fan   3. wizard   4. voice
5. dragon   6. spell   7. mirror   8. dark
9. rushes   10. holds   11. becomes

Ⓔ A Gift from Harry   p.49

Lucy loves to read *Harry Potter*.

One night, a white owl appears in her m<u>irror</u>.

Lucy <u>asks</u> the owl <u>for</u> help.

"Can you take me to Hogwarts?" Lucy falls into the mirror.

Lucy meets Harry, so she <u>becomes</u> excited.

"I'm your biggest <u>fan</u>. How can I become a w<u>izard</u>?"

Harry says, "Shh, don't speak in a loud <u>voice</u>. Come with me."

Harry opens the door in the d<u>ark</u>.

A <u>dragon</u> is flying in the night sky.

He says the spell, "Incendio, locomoter."

A fire starts, and it <u>rushes</u> into the dragon's mouth.

Lucy says, "You are so br<u>ave</u>. I want to learn your s<u>pells</u>."

Harry says, "Let me give you this spell list."

Lucy wakes up <u>holding</u> a spell book in her hand.

Lucy goes out and shouts, "Incendio!"

● 해석 ●

해리의 선물

루시는 '해리포터' 읽는 것을 아주 좋아한다.

어느 날 밤, 흰 부엉이가 그녀의 거울에 나타난다.

루시는 부엉이에게 도움을 요청한다.

"나를 호크와트에 데려다 줄래?" 루시는 거울 속으로 빠진다.

루시는 해리를 만나서 흥분한다.

"나는 너의 최고의 팬이야. 어떻게 하면 내가 마법사가 될 수 있니?"

해리가 말한다. "쉿, 큰 소리로 말하지마. 날 따라와."

해리는 어둠 속에서 문을 연다.

용이 밤하늘을 날아간다.

해리는 주문을 건다. "인센디오, 로코모토르."

붙이 ㅣ ㅏ 타 ㅣ 서 용이 입 속으로 돌진한다.

루시가 말한다. "너는 매우 용감하구나. 나도 너의 주문을 배우고 싶어."

해리가 말한다. "내가 너에게 이 주문 목록을 줄게."

루시는 손에 주문 책을 쥔 채로 깨어난다.

루시는 밖으로 나가서 외친다. "인센디오!"

Unit 6

About Cars
차에 대하여

• Lesson 1 • Ford Model T   p.50

Ⓐ
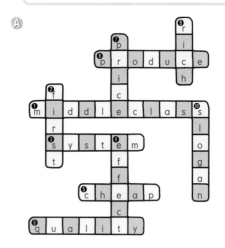

▶▶ ACROSS

❶ middle class   ❸ system   ❺ cheap
❻ quality   ❽ produce

▼ DOWN

❷ first   ❹ effect   ❼ price   ❾ rich
❿ slogan

Ⓑ
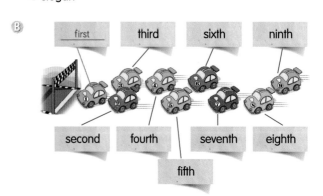

first   third   sixth   ninth
second   fourth   seventh   eighth
fifth

Ⓒ 1. low   2. rich   3. slogan   4. first

Ⓓ 1. mass   2. system   3. middle class
4. effect   5. produce   6. quality   7. price
8. cheap

Ⓔ Ford Model T   p.53

Watch the Ford go by.
"HIGH Q<u>UALITY</u> IN A <u>LOW</u>-PRICED CAR"
This was the poster <u>slogan</u> of the Ford Model T in 1909.
Henry Ford <u>produced</u> the Ford Model T from 1908 to 1927.
Ford made the car with a new s<u>ystem</u>, the assembly line.
The Ford Model T was the first car <u>mass</u>-produced on an
assembly line.
It was so <u>cheap</u> that ordinary people could afford it.
Before the Ford Model T, the <u>prices</u> of cars were very
expensive.
So only <u>rich</u> people could buy cars at that time.
After the Ford Model T, cars became popular.
The car made traveling easy for <u>middle class</u> Americans.
Ford had an important e<u>ffect</u> on people's lives.
That's why the Model T is called "the <u>first</u> people's car."

● 해석 ●
포드 모델 T
포드 차가 지나가는 것을 보세요.
"낮은 가격의 고품질의 차"
이것은 1909년 포드 자동차 모델 T의 포스터 표어였다.
헨리 포드는 1908년부터 1927년까지 포드 모델 T를 생산했다.
포드는 조립라인이라는 새로운 방식으로 차를 만들었다.
포드 모델 T는 조립라인에서 대량으로 생산된 첫 번째 차였다.
그 차는 무척 싸서 일반 사람들도 살 수 있었다.
포드 모델 T가 나오기 전에는 자동차 가격들이 매우 비쌌다.
그래서 오직 부자들만이 그 당시에 자동차를 살 수 있었다.
포드 모델 T가 나온 이후에 자동차는 대중적이 되었다.
그 자동차는 중산층의 미국 사람들이 쉽게 여행하는 것을 가능하게 해주
었다.
포드는 사람들의 삶에 중요한 영향을 주었다.
그것이 모델 T가 '대중의 첫 번째 자동차'라고 불리는 이유이다.

• Lesson 2 • **A Flying Car**   p.54

Ⓐ

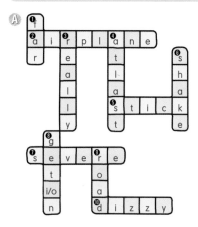

▶▶▶ ACROSS
❷ airplane   ❺ stick   ❼ severe   ❿ dizzy

⬇ DOWN
❶ far   ❸ really   ❹ at last   ❻ shake
❽ get in[on]   ❾ road

Ⓑ 1. traffic jam   2. happened   3. get on

Ⓒ 1. stuck   2. had   3. paid   4. got

Ⓓ 1. shakes   2. severe   3. far   4. road
5. airplane   6. At last   7. get   8. stuck
9. dizzy   10. really

Ⓔ A Flying Car   p.57

Many cars are on the <u>road</u>.
"There's a <u>traffic jam</u>. It's s<u>evere</u>.
We're <u>stuck</u> on the road," says Lucy's dad.
"We're too <u>far</u> from home.
I need a flying car. Abracadabra!" says Lucy.
Then, a flying car lands on the road.
Lucy and her dad <u>get</u> in the flying car.
The flying car flies up into the sky.
However, the flying car begins to sh<u>ake</u>.
"Dad, what is <u>happening</u>? I feel <u>dizzy</u>."
"Lucy, don't worry. An <u>airplane</u> flew past us."
<u>At</u> <u>last</u>, they arrive at home.
"Wow! We're home. That was r<u>eally</u> fast!"

● 해석 ●
날아가는 차
많은 차들이 길 위에 있다.
"교통 체증이네. 심각하군. 우리는 길 위에 갇혔어."라고 루시 아빠가 말한다.

"우리는 집에서 너무 멀리 있어요. 날아가는 차가 필요해요. 아브라카다
브라!" 루시가 말한다 그러자, 날아가는 차가 두루 위에 착륙한다
루시와 아빠는 날아가는 차를 탄다.
날아가는 차가 하늘로 날아 올라간다.
그러나, 날아가는 차가 흔들리기 시작한다.
"아빠, 무슨 일이에요? 저 어지러워요."
"루시야, 걱정 마. 비행기가 우리 옆을 지나갔어."
마침내 그들은 집에 도착한다.
"와! 집에 왔다. 그거 정말 빨랐어!"

Unit 7
At the Beach
해변에서

• Lesson 1 • **Boracay Beach**   p.58

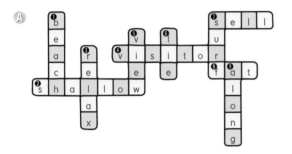

▶▶▶ ACROSS

❷ shallow   ❹ visitor   ❼ sell   ❽ fat

▾ DOWN

❶ beach   ❸ relax   ❺ view   ❻ lie

❼ surf   ❾ along

Ⓑ 1. beach   2. sandcastles   3. surfs   4. water fights

Ⓒ 1. sells   2. fat   3. beach   4. water fight

Ⓓ 1. relax   2. visitors   3. view   4. along

5. surf   6. shallow   7. lie   8. sandcastles

Ⓔ **Boracay Beach**   p.61

Boracay Beach is in the Philippines.
The beach is famous for its lovely views.
Many people visit and relax on the beach.
Visitors can enjoy many things at the beach.
A woman lies in the sun and enjoys the sunshine.
A girl wearing a bikini walks along the beach.
A man sells ice cream under a large parasol.

A fat woman searches for shells.
A boy builds a sandcastle.
Some kids have a water fight.
Little kids play in the shallow water.
Some people surf the waves in the sea.

● 해석 ●
보라카이 해변
보라카이 해변은 필리핀에 있다.
그 해변은 멋진 경치로 유명하다.
많은 사람들이 그 해변을 방문해서 휴식을 취한다.
방문객들은 해변에서 많은 것들을 즐길 수 있다.
여자가 태양 아래에 누워서 햇볕을 즐기고 있다.
비키니를 입은 소녀가 해변을 따라 걷고 있다.
남자가 큰 파라솔 밑에서 아이스크림을 팔고 있다.
뚱뚱한 여자가 조개 껍질들을 찾는다.
소년이 모래성을 만든다.
몇몇 아이들은 물싸움을 한다.
어린 꼬마들이 얕은 물에서 놀고 있다.
몇몇 사람들은 바다에서 파도타기를 한다.

• Lesson 2 • **Hi, Mr. Dolphin**   p.62

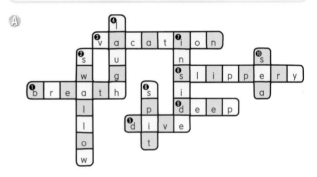

▶▶▶ ACROSS

❶ breath   ❸ vacation   ❺ dive   ❽ slippery

❾ deep

▾ DOWN

❷ swallow   ❹ laugh   ❻ spit   ❼ inside

❿ sea

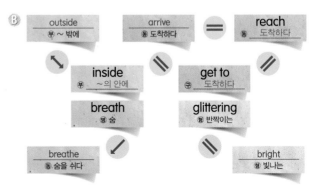

ⓒ 1. laughs　　2. laughs at　　3. laugh　　4. laugh at

ⓓ 1. vacation　　2. sea　　3. deep　　4. glittering
　 5. breath　　6. swallows　　7. spits　　8. inside
　 9. slippery　　10. dives

ⓔ Hi, Mr. Dolphin　p.65

Lucy's family goes on a summer <u>vacation</u> to the beach.
Her dad drives to <u>get to</u> the beach.
Lucy wants to explore under the <u>sea</u>.
She wears goggles and <u>dives</u> into the sea.
She holds her b<u>reath</u> underwater.
"Look at the colorful fish. They are g<u>littering</u>."
She swims d<u>eeper</u> into the sea.
A dolphin <u>swallows</u> Lucy in its big mouth.
She shouts, "Ahhhhh! What happened?
It's really dark and s<u>lippery</u>."
She is <u>inside</u> the dolphin.
She jumps up and down.
"I don't like it here."
The dolphin <u>spits</u> her out.
"Oh! It's you, Mr. Dolphin!"
Mr. Dolphin <u>laughs</u>.

● 해석 ●
안녕, 미스터 돌고래
루시의 가족이 해변으로 여름 휴가를 간다.
그녀의 아빠가 운전해서 해변에 도착한다.
루시는 바다 밑을 탐험하고 싶다.
그녀는 물안경을 쓰고 바다로 잠수한다.
그녀는 물속에서 숨을 참는다.
"화려한 물고기들을 봐. 반짝거려."
그녀는 바다 속으로 더 깊이 수영한다.
돌고래 한 마리가 큰 입으로 루시를 삼킨다.
그녀가 소리친다. "아! 무슨 일이지?
정말 어둡고 미끄럽네."
그녀는 돌고래 안에 있다.
그녀는 위아래로 점프를 한다.
"나는 여기가 싫어."
돌고래가 그녀를 뱉는다.
"아! 당신이었군요, 미스터 돌고래!"
미스터 돌고래가 웃는다.

Unit 8
I Enjoy Cooking
나는 요리를 즐겨요

• Lesson 1 • How to Make Chicken Curry　p.66

ⓐ

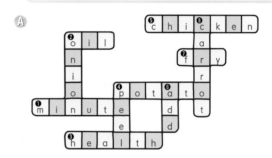

▶▶▶ ACROSS

❶ minute　　❷ oil　　❸ health　　❹ potato
❺ chicken　　❼ fry

⬇ DOWN

❷ onion　　❹ peel　　❻ add　　❽ carrot

ⓑ 1. how to　　2. ingredients　　3. potatoes　　4. peels

ⓒ 1. carrots　　2. peels　　3. potato　　4. chicken

ⓓ 1. ingredients　2. peel　　3. Fry　　4. oil
　 5. minutes　　6. how to　　7. Add　　8. health

ⓔ How to Make Chicken Curry　p.69

Curry is good for our <u>health</u>.
Let's make a delicious chicken curry for four people.
Take a look.

<u>Ingredients</u>:
· <u>oil</u>
· one <u>onion</u> and one <u>carrot</u>
· two <u>potatoes</u>
· 400 g <u>chicken</u>
· curry powder
· 400~450 ml water

<u>How to</u> Make:
First, <u>peel</u> an onion and the other vegetables.
Second, cut up the potatoes, carrot, and onion.
Third, put them in a pan and <u>fry</u> them in oil.
After that, put the chicken in and cook everything together.

Finally, <u>add</u> the curry powder and water.
Cook for 40 <u>minutes</u>.

● 해석 ●

치킨카레를 만드는 법

카레는 우리의 건강에 좋다.
4인분을 위한 맛있는 치킨카레를 만들어 보자.
다음을 살펴보자.

재료:
· 기름
· 양파 한 개와 당근 한 개
· 감자 두 개
· 닭고기 400 그램
· 카레 가루
· 물 400 ~ 450 밀리리터

만드는 법:
첫째, 양파와 다른 채소의 껍질을 벗겨라.
둘째, 감자, 당근, 양파를 잘라라.
셋째, 그것들을 팬에 넣고 기름에 볶아라.
그러고 나서, 닭고기를 넣고 모든 것을 함께 요리해라.
마지막으로, 카레 가루와 물을 넣어라.
40분 동안 요리해라.

● Lesson 2 ● **Giggle Gaggle Cooking Contest** p.70

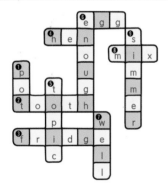

▶▶ ACROSS

❷ tooth　❸ fridge　❹ hen　❻ egg
❽ mix

▽ DOWN

❶ pot　❺ topic　❻ enough　❼ well
❾ simmer

Ⓒ 1. happy　2. happier　3. happiest

Ⓓ 1. chef　2. well　3. topic　4. enough
5. hen　6. pot　7. simmers　8. eggs
9. fridge　10. mixes　11. teeth

Ⓔ **Giggle Gaggle Cooking Contest** p.73

Topic: The Happiest Meal
Day: July 7
Prize: A Free Airline Ticket to France
Lucy and Mr. Cook want to join the cooking contest.
Mr. Cook is a great <u>chef</u>.
He cooks very <u>well</u>.
They prepare some ingredients for the h<u>appiest</u> meal.
Lucy looks in the <u>fridge</u> to get some ingredients.
She takes out one <u>egg</u>, some potatoes, and some carrots.
Mr. Cook says, "It's not <u>enough</u>. We need something more."
He gets a goldfish's <u>tooth</u> and some h<u>en</u>'s feet.
They put them in the <u>pot</u>.
"Let's <u>mix</u> them together," says Mr. Cook.
"Let's <u>simmer</u> them," says Lucy.
They finish cooking.
"Let's taste it. Wow! It's yummy. I am so happy."
"We will win the contest."

● 해석 ●

낄낄 깔깔 요리대회

주제: 가장 행복한 음식
날짜: 7월 7일
상: 프랑스행 무료 비행기 티켓
루시와 미스터 쿡은 요리대회에 참여하고 싶다.
미스터 쿡은 훌륭한 주방장이다.
그는 요리를 매우 잘한다.
그들은 가장 행복한 음식을 만들기 위해 재료들을 준비한다.
루시는 재료를 얻기 위해 냉장고 안을 살펴본다.
그녀는 달걀 한 개, 몇 개의 감자와 당근을 꺼낸다.

미스터 쿡이 말한다. "이것으론 충분하지 않아. 우린 뭔가 더 필요해."
그는 금붕어의 이빨과 암탉의 발을 좀 가져온다.
그들은 그것들을 냄비에 담는다.
"그것들을 함께 섞자." 미스터 쿡이 말한다.
"그것들을 끓여요." 루시가 말한다.
그들은 요리를 끝낸다.
"맛을 보자. 맛있어. 와! 나는 정말 행복해."
"우리는 대회에서 우승할 거예요."

Unit 9
At the Hospital
병원에서

• Lesson 1 • In the Emergency Room p.74

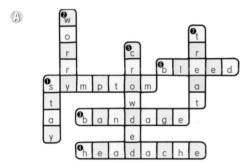

▶▶▶ ACROSS

❶ symptom   ❸ bandage   ❹ headache   ❻ bleed

⬇ DOWN

❶ stay   ❷ worry   ❺ crowded   ❼ treat

Ⓑ 1. patient   2. hospital   3. emergency   4. treats

Ⓒ 1. headache   2. bandage   3. emergency   4. hurt

Ⓓ 1. hospital   2. crowded   3. patient   4. symptoms
5. bleeds   6. stay   7. worry   8. treat

Ⓔ In the Emergency Room   p.77

Sick people go to the <u>hospital</u>.
The <u>emergency</u> room (ER) is busy all day.
It is open 24 hours a day.
It is the most <u>crowded</u> place in the hospital.
A boy who has a <u>h</u>eadache is crying.
His mother <u>worries</u> about him.
A b<u>leeding</u> man is carried in on a stretcher from the ambulance.

He <u>hurt</u> his arm. A nurse puts a <u>bandage</u> on his arm.
Doctors and nurses <u>s</u>tay there all day.
They are always busy taking care of <u>patients</u>.
Sick people have different kinds of sy<u>mptoms</u>.
Doctors and nurses <u>treat</u> them in different ways.
Lots of lives are saved in the ER.

● 해석 ●

응급실에서
아픈 사람들은 병원에 간다.
응급실은 하루 종일 붐빈다.
그곳은 하루 24시간 열려 있다.
그곳은 병원에서 가장 혼잡한 장소이다.
머리가 아픈 소년이 울고 있다.
그의 엄마는 그를 걱정한다.
피를 흘리는 남자가 앰뷸런스에서 들것에 실려 온다.
그는 팔을 다쳤다. 간호사가 그의 팔에 붕대를 감아준다.
의사들과 간호사들은 하루 종일 그곳에 머무른다.
그들은 환자들을 돌보느라 항상 바쁘다.
아픈 사람들은 다른 종류의 증상들을 갖고 있다.
의사와 간호사는 다른 방법들로 그들을 치료한다.
많은 생명들이 응급실에서 구해진다.

• Lesson 2 • Lucy Becomes a Doctor p.78

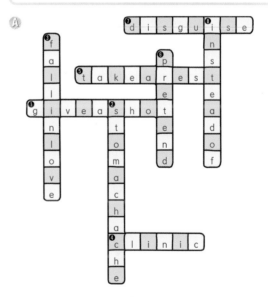

▶▶▶ ACROSS

❶ give a shot   ❹ clinic   ❺ take a rest
❼ disguise

⬇ DOWN

❷ stomachache   ❸ fall in love   ❻ pretend
❽ instead of

B

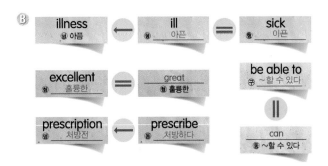

illness 명 아픔 ← ill 형 아픈 = sick 형 아픈

excellent 형 훌륭한 = great 형 훌륭한

be able to ⊕ ~할 수 있다

prescription 명 처방전 ← prescribe 통 처방하다

|| can 통 ~할 수 있다

루시는 그녀에게 주사를 놓아 주었는데, 그러자 그녀의 기분이 나아졌다.
루시는 또한 그녀에게 휴식을 취하라고 말했다.
그녀는 의사로서 훌륭하게 잘 해냈다.

C 1. stomachache 2. headache 3. toothache

D 1. excellent 2. clinic 3. ill 4. pretends
5. be able to 6. falls in love 7. disguises 8. take a rest
9. Instead of 10. prescribes 11. gives, a shot

E Lucy Becomes a Doctor p.81

Lucy's father is a doctor.
One day, he got sick and wasn't <u>able</u> to go to work.
Lucy decided to go to work <u>instead of</u> her father.
She <u>disguised</u> herself as a doctor.
When she wore a white coat, she looked like her father.
A boy came to the <u>clinic</u> with his mother.
He p<u>retended</u> to be <u>ill</u> because he didn't want to go to school.
"I have a <u>stomachache</u>," said the boy.
Lucy <u>prescribed</u> the boy some fake medicine.
The next patient was a man who <u>fell in love</u>.
Lucy told him to stand on his head for 5 minutes.
She thought it would stop him for thinking about her.
A woman who felt blue came to Lucy.
Lucy <u>gave</u> her <u>a shot</u>, which made her feel better.
Lucy also told her to <u>take a rest</u>.
She did an <u>excellent</u> job as a doctor.

● 해석 ●
루시가 의사가 된다
루시의 아빠는 의사이다.
어느 날, 그는 아파서 일을 하러 갈 수 없었다.
루시는 아빠 대신에 일하러 가기로 결심했다.
그녀는 의사로 변장했다.
그녀가 흰 가운을 입으니 아빠처럼 보였다.
한 소년이 엄마와 함께 병원에 왔다.
그는 학교에 가기 싫어서 아픈 척했다.
"배가 아파요."라고 소년이 말했다.
루시는 소년에게 가짜 약을 좀 처방했다.
다음 환자는 사랑에 빠진 남자였다.
루시는 그에게 5분 동안 물구나무 서 있으라고 말했다.
그녀는 그것이 그가 그녀에 대해 생각하는 일을 멈추게 해줄 거라고 생각했다.
기분이 우울한 여자가 루시에게 왔다.

Unit 10 Roller Coaster 롤러코스터

● Lesson 1 ● **Why Do People Like Roller Coasters?** p.82

A

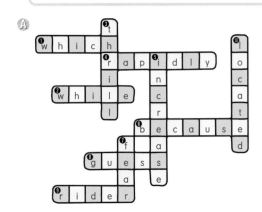

▶▶▶ ACROSS
❶ which ❷ while ❹ rapidly ❻ because
❽ guess ❾ rider

⬇ DOWN
❸ thrill ❺ increase ❼ fear ❿ located

B 1. top 2. at the same time 3. thrill, fear

C 1. top 2. fear 3. Which 4. rapidly

D 1. located 2. thrilled 3. increased
4. Guess 5. because 6. while 7. riders
8. at the same tIme

E Why Do People Like Roller Coasters? p.85

People like to ride roller coasters.
Can you <u>guess</u> the reason?
It's <u>because</u> the speed makes people excited.
Roller coasters go slowly to the <u>top</u>.
The r<u>iders</u> feel excited and nervous w<u>hile</u> it's going up to the top.
The roller coaster <u>which</u> reaches the top goes down ra<u>pidly</u>.

The speed of the roller coaster <u>increases</u>.
A sudden change in speed makes people get a <u>thrill</u>.
Also they feel <u>fear</u>.
They experience two feelings <u>at</u> <u>the</u> <u>same</u> <u>time</u>.
What is the fastest roller coaster in the world?
It's Formular Rossa, <u>located</u> at Ferrari World in the United Arab Emirates.
People from all over the world go there to ride it.

● 해석 ●

왜 사람들은 롤러 코스터를 좋아할까?
사람들은 롤러 코스터 타는 것을 좋아한다.
당신은 그 이유를 추측할 수 있는가?
그것은 속도가 사람들을 흥분시키기 때문이다.
롤러 코스터는 꼭대기까지 천천히 간다.
탑승자들은 그것이 꼭대기까지 올라가는 동안 흥분하고 긴장한다.
꼭대기에 도달한 롤러 코스터는 급격하게 떨어진다.
롤러 코스터의 속도가 증가한다.
갑작스런 속도의 변화는 사람들이 전율을 느끼게 한다.
또한 그들은 공포를 느낀다.
그들은 동시에 두 가지 감정을 경험한다.
세상에서 가장 빠른 롤러 코스터는 무엇일까?
그것은 아랍 에미레이트 공화국에 있는 페라리 월드에 위치한 포뮬라 로사이다.
전세계에서 온 사람들이 그것을 타기 위해 그곳에 간다.

• Lesson 2 • **An Adventure with a Genie** p.86

Ⓐ
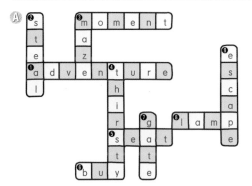

▶▶ ACROSS

❶ adventure   ❸ moment   ❺ seat   ❻ buy
❽ lamp

⬇ DOWN

❷ steal   ❸ maze   ❹ thirsty   ❼ gate
❾ escape

Ⓑ

| adventure 형 모험 | → | adventurous 형 모험심이 강한 |
| imagine 동 상상하다 | → | imagination 형 상상, 상상력 |

| yesterday 형 어제 | ← | today 형 오늘 | → | tomorrow 형 내일 |

Ⓒ 1. seatbelt   2. window seat   3. aisle seat

Ⓓ 1. lamp   2. adventure   3. Yesterday   4. bought
5. imagines   6. maze   7. steals   8. thirsty
9. gate   10. escapes   11. moment

Ⓔ **An Adventure with a Genie**   p.89

Lucy went to the amusement park <u>yesterday</u>.
Lucy felt <u>thirsty</u>.
So Lucy <u>bought</u> a bottle of water and drank it.
"You can get what you <u>imagine</u> if you drink this," was written on the bottle. Lucy rode on the roller coaster.
Lucy thought about Aladdin's magic <u>lamp</u>.
Then, a magic lamp and a genie appeared in Lucy's hand. And a wizard appeared in the back s<u>eat</u>.
He tried to st<u>eal</u> the lamp.
Lucy and the genie went into the m<u>aze</u>.
But Lucy wanted to <u>escape</u> from the maze.
"Find the <u>gate</u>, please, Genie," said Lucy.
At that <u>moment</u>, Lucy appeared on the outside of the gate.
The genie said, "Goodbye. It's time to go home."
Lucy went home and told her family about her <u>adventure</u> with the genie.

● 해석 ●

지니와 함께 한 모험
루시는 어제 놀이동산에 갔다.
루시는 목이 말랐다.
그래서 루시는 물 한 병을 사서 마셨다.
'이 물을 마시면 당신이 상상한 것을 얻을 수 있다.'라고 물병에 쓰여 있었다.
루시는 롤러 코스터를 탔다.
루시는 알라딘의 요술 램프를 생각했다.
그때, 요술 램프와 지니가 루시의 손에 나타났다. 그리고 뒷좌석에 마법사가 나타났다.
그는 그 램프를 훔치려고 했다.
루시와 지니는 미로로 갔다.
하지만 루시는 미로에서 탈출하고 싶었다.
"지니, 제발 출구를 찾아 줘." 루시가 말했다.
그 순간 루시는 출입문 밖에 나타났다.
지니가 "잘 가. 집에 갈 시간이야."라고 말했다.
루시는 집에 가서 가족에게 지니와 함께한 모험에 대해 말해주었다.

Wow! Smart Vocabulary

보너스 지식이 팡팡!
케이블카 타는 것보다 재미있는
블루베리 껌보다 맛있는 책 (**이혜린** 서현초 3학년)
러(너)와 나 함께
리(이)야기 속 단어 공부 여행 떠나보자
(임서영 탄천초 4학년)

보며 신나는 지식
케이스에 소중하게 담아두는 지식
블럭처럼 쌓아가는 우리의 지식 (**장서연** 서현초 3학년)
러(너)와 나의 지식이야
리(이) 책을 펼쳐봐, 엄청난 지식이 쏟아질 거야
(황인태 서현초 3학년)

와우, 영어 공부 하기에 정말 좋아요
우와, 더욱 자세히 나와 있네요
스마트한 영어 공부법
마트에는 없어요~ 서점으로 오세요
트러블이 영어이신 분, 이제 쉽게 공부할 수 있어요
(박지수 용마초 5학년)

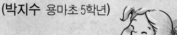

보르르 떨며
케케케 웃으며
블링블링 읽는
러브레터처럼
리얼한 이 책
(맹재형 서현초 3학년)

보아야 후회 안 되는
케첩처럼 톡톡 튀는 (**천사랑** 용마초 5학년)
블럭 버스터의 숨막히는 장면처럼
러블리한 영어 단어들
리(이)야기로 공부하면 모두 내 것이 되지
(장우혁 탄천초 6학년)

와우~ 재미있는 이야기가 가득!
우리들이 쉽게 읽을 수 있는 즐거운 스토리
스마트한 영단어를
마구마구 쏙쏙 집어넣은 이야기
트집잡을 게 없는 완벽한 교재야!
(민동안 용마초 6학년)

보물섬 같은 영어의 세계
케케묵은 단어 외우기 공부 말고
블랙홀처럼 모든 단어를 빨아들이는 방법 없을까?
러(너)무 고민하지마~
리(이) 책으로
이야기와 함께 공부하면 고민 해결!
(신하진 탄천초 4학년)

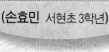

보고 또 봐도 질리지 않고
케이크처럼 달고
블루베리보다 좋아 (**박정은** 서현초 3학년)
러브하고 싶을 정도
리(이)렇게 재밌는 책은 처음이에요
(손효민 서현초 3학년)

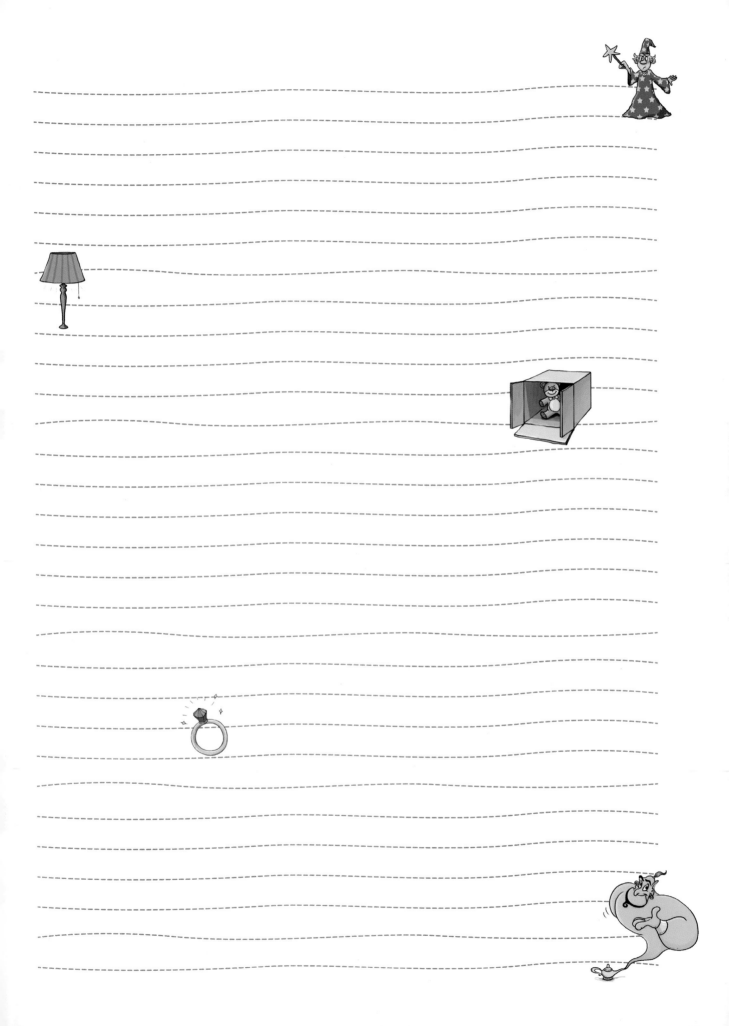

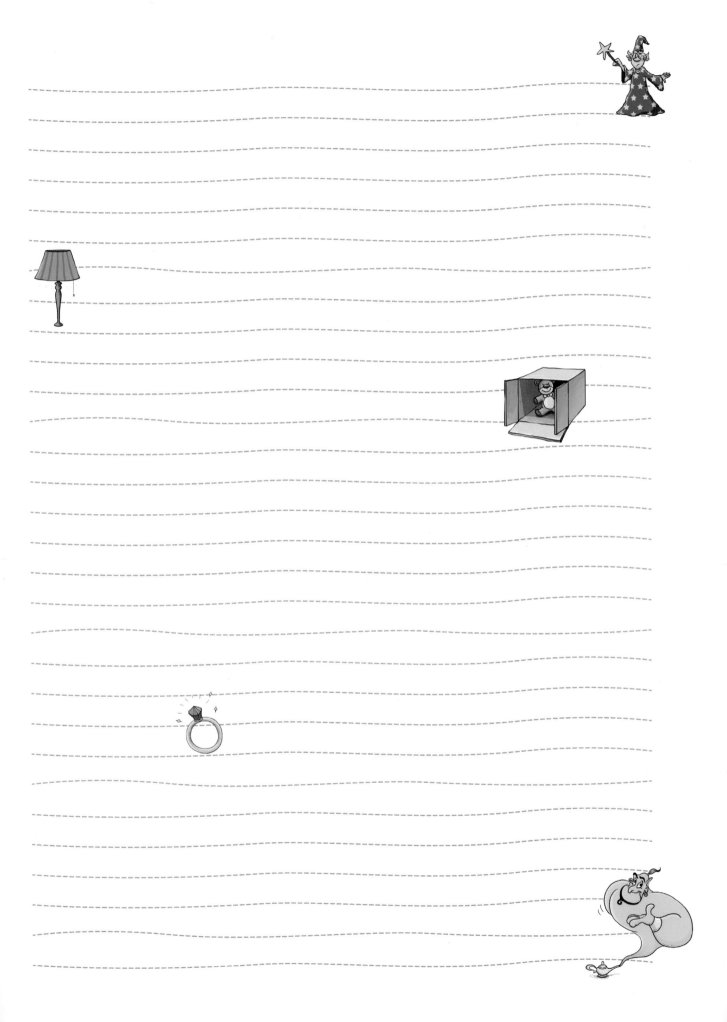

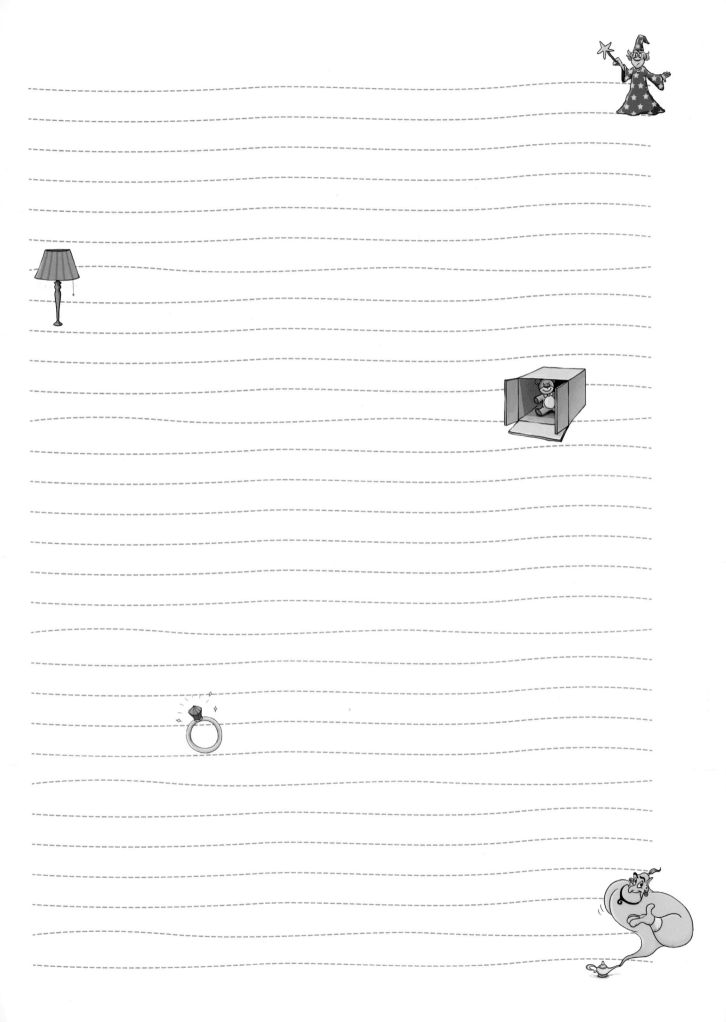

WOW! Smart Grammar

전 3권 시리즈

스토리를 타고 흐르는 기본 핵심 영문법!

⭐ 흥미로운 스토리에 기반한 생생한 예문과 체계적인 연습문제

⭐ 다양한 유형의 3단계 연습문제 Quiz Time

⭐ 중학교 시험·공인 영어 시험 대비도 OK! Review Test

⭐ 부담 없이 익히는 영어권 문화 상식 Super Duper Fun Time

⭐ 스마트한 자기주도학습의 파트너, 워크북 & 휴대용 단어장

⭐ 책 속의 영어문장 해석 무료 다운로드 www.darakwon.co.kr

다락원

wow! Smart Vocabulary ③

워크북

Unit 1

My Collection

A 다음 단어들의 우리말 뜻을 모두 알고 있나요? 확인해 보세요.

단어의 품사에 맞는 우리말 뜻을 쓰세요.

1. ☐ money 명	13. ☐ with 전
2. ☐ when 접 부	14. ☐ always 부
3. ☐ world 명	15. ☐ nap 명
4. ☐ collect 동	16. ☐ hug 동
5. ☐ map 명	17. ☐ cloudy 형
6. ☐ coin 명	18. ☐ light 명 형
7. ☐ face 명	19. ☐ where 부 접
8. ☐ represent 동	20. ☐ contest 명
9. ☐ bill 명	21. ☐ alive 형
10. ☐ scrapbook 명	22. ☐ stage 명
11. ☐ wrinkle 동	23. ☐ prize 명
12. ☐ memory 명	24. ☐ proud 형

B 우리말과 같은 뜻이 되도록 빈칸을 채워 영어 문장을 완성하세요.

1.	이것은 나의 돈 수집품이다.	This is my _____ collection.
2.	나는 여행할 때 사진을 많이 찍는다.	I take many pictures _____ I travel.
3.	나는 전세계를 여행할 것이다.	I will travel all over the _____.

2

4.	나는 나의 여행을 기억하기 위해 돈을 수집한다.	I money to remember my trips.
5.	내 펜들이 세계지도 위에 있다.	My pens are on my world .
6.	동전들이 달라 보인다.	The look different.
7.	그것들에는 위인들의 얼굴이 있다.	There are great people's on them.
8.	또한 각 나라를 대표하는 것들도 있다.	Things that each country are on them, too.
9.	지폐는 특수한 종이로 만든다.	are made of a special kind of paper.
10.	나는 그것들을 스크랩북에 넣는다.	I put them in a .
11.	그래서 그것들은 구겨지지 않을 것이다.	So, they will not get .
12.	나는 내 수집품을 볼 때마다 여행의 추억들을 생각한다.	Whenever I see my collection, I think about my from my trips.
13.	루시는 그녀의 인형들과 노는 것을 좋아한다.	Lucy likes playing her dolls.
14.	그녀는 언제나 그것들을 가지고 다닌다.	She brings them with her.
15.	어느 날, 그녀는 소파에서 낮잠을 잔다.	One day, she takes a on the sofa.
16.	그녀는 그녀의 인형을 안고 있다.	She is her doll.
17.	그녀의 꿈 속에는 구름이 잔뜩 끼어 있다.	It's so in her dream.
18.	갑자기 빛이 나고, 그녀는 눈을 뜰 수가 없다.	Suddenly, there is a , but she can't open her eyes.
19.	그녀는 그녀가 어디에 있는 지 믿을 수가 없다.	She can't believe she is.
20.	이곳은 블라이스 인형 모델 대회이다.	It's a Blythe doll modeling .
21.	모든 인형들이 살아 있고 멋있어 보인다.	All the dolls are and look wonderful.
22.	그녀가 가장 좋아하는 블라이스 인형이 무대 위에 있다.	Her favorite Blythe doll is on the .
23.	그녀는 1등을 해서 왕관을 쓴다.	She wins first and wears the crown.
24.	루시는 그녀가 정말 자랑스럽다.	Lucy is so of her.

A 빈칸에 어울리는 단어를 고르세요.

1. I like _____ stamps. It's one of my hobbies.
   ① collecting ② cooking ③ calling ④ caring

2. The trips live in my _____. They were so impressive.
   ① meaning ② melon ③ memory ④ meeting

3. Turn on the _____. I don't want to be in a dark room.
   ① life ② loss ③ lemon ④ light

4. I put some _____ in the vending machine. I want a Coke so I push the Coke button.
   ① cold ② cats ③ coins ④ cars

5. He will attend a taekwondo _____. He's good at taekwondo.
   ① contest ② career ③ collect ④ clown

6. These pants _____ easily. They need to be ironed.
   ① wrist ② wrinkle ③ watch ④ wallet

7. She gets sleepy after lunch. So, she takes a _____.
   ① now ② nap ③ nut ④ net

8. Paul sleeps _____ his mother at night. He doesn't like to sleep alone.
   ① over ② under ③ without ④ with

9. Actors are performing a play. All of them are on the _____.
   ① state ② skip ③ stage ④ star

10. I can lend you some _____. How much do you need?
    ① money ② monkey ③ mommy ④ monster

11. There are a few moles on her _____. Most of them are on her cheeks.
    ① father ② fall ③ face ④ feeling

12. Do you have a _____ of Jeju? I wonder where Mt. Halla is.
① man ② mon ③ mop ④ map

13. _____ is your birthday? Is it in May?
① Where ② When ③ Why ④ Who

14. Come on, dear. Give me a _____.
① hug ② home ③ hire ④ hate

15. It's dark and _____ outside. It looks like it's going to rain.
① cloudy ② closed ③ clean ④ clear

B 밑줄 친 단어와 비슷한 뜻을 가진 단어를 고르세요.

16. She travels around the <u>world</u> with her father.
① university ② universe ③ uncle ④ union

17. You're <u>always</u> late for school.
① all the way ② all the time ③ all the things ④ all time

18. The Korean team won a <u>prize</u> in the baseball game.
① award ② animal ③ aunt ④ arm

19. The symbol <u>represents</u> our city.
① starts from ② stays up ③ stands up ④ stands for

C 밑줄 친 단어와 반대되는 뜻을 가진 단어를 고르세요.

20. I can't believe that the robot is <u>alive</u>. It's walking this way.
① deep ② dear ③ dead ④ dark

Score: ___ /20

Amazing B-Boy Dancers

Word Check

A 다음 단어들의 우리말 뜻을 모두 알고 있나요? 확인해 보세요.

> 단어의 품사에 맞는 우리말 뜻을 쓰세요.

1.	☐ dance	동 / 명	13.	☐ perform	동
2.	☐ teenager	명	14.	☐ role	명
3.	☐ amazing	형	15.	☐ partner	명
4.	☐ spin	동	16.	☐ street	명
5.	☐ speed	명	17.	☐ handsome	형
6.	☐ another	형	18.	☐ pull	동
7.	☐ support	동	19.	☐ fantastic	형
8.	☐ give a big hand	구	20.	☐ prince	명
9.	☐ hard	부 / 형	21.	☐ swim	동
10.	☐ every	형	22.	☐ appear	동
11.	☐ great	형	23.	☐ go down on one's knees	구
12.	☐ pleased	형	24.	☐ together	부

B 우리말과 같은 뜻이 되도록 빈칸을 채워 영어 문장을 완성하세요.

1.	여러분은 비보이 춤들을 좋아하는가?	Do you like B-boy ?
2.	그 노래는 요즘 십대들 사이에서 인기가 있다.	The song is popular among these days.
3.	그들은 정말 놀랍다.	They are really .

4.	한 비보이 댄서가 돌고 있다.	One B-boy dancer .
5.	그는 빠른 속도로 돌고 있다.	He spins at high .
6.	다른 비보이 댄서를 보라.	Look at B-boy dancer.
7.	그는 오직 한 팔로 몸을 지탱한다.	He his body with only one arm.
8.	사람들은 그들이 노래하는 것을 보고 큰 박수를 보내고 있다.	People watch them sing and them .
9.	그들은 정말 열심히 연습한다.	They practice really .
10.	매년, 영국 챔피언십이 열린다.	year, the U.K. Championship is held.
11.	그들은 정말 대단해서 많은 상을 탔다.	They were so that they won many prizes.
12.	많은 팬들은 그들의 성공 소식을 듣고서 기뻐했다.	Many fans were to hear about their success.
13.	루시는 백조의 호수를 공연할 것이다.	Lucy is going to *Swan Lake*.
14.	그녀는 오데뜨 역할을 맡는다.	She takes the of Odette.
15.	그러나 그녀는 아직 댄스 파트너가 없다.	But she has no dance yet.
16.	어느 날, 루시는 길거리 댄스 공연을 본다.	One day, Lucy sees a dance performance.
17.	잘생긴 비보이 댄서가 루시의 손을 잡는다.	A B-boy dancer grabs Lucy's hand.
18.	그는 그녀를 무대 위로 잡아당긴다.	He her up on stage.
19.	갑자기, 그녀는 환상적인 세계로 떨어진다.	Suddenly, she falls into a world.
20.	비보이 댄서가 왕자로 변한다.	The B-boy dancer changes into a .
21.	루시도 백조가 되어 호수에서 수영을 한다.	Lucy becomes a swan and in the lake, too.
22.	갑자기, 잘생긴 비보이 왕자가 나타난다.	Suddenly, the handsome B-boy prince .
23.	그는 한쪽 무릎을 꿇고 그녀에게 프로포즈를 한다.	He and proposes to her.
24.	그들은 달빛 아래서 함께 춤을 춘다.	They dance under the moonlight.

Review Test

Ⓐ 빈칸에 어울리는 단어를 고르세요.

1. Let's do this work _____. Many hands make light work.
   ① thin ② thick ③ together ④ tall

2. Which baseball team do you _____? I cheer for New York.
   ① succeed ② support ③ sing ④ suppose

3. He is a hard worker. He gets up at 6 o'clock _____ day and sweeps the yard.
   ① emotional ② ever ③ even ④ every

4. This road has a _____ limit. Don't drive over 60 km per hour.
   ① skill ② stage ③ speed ④ star

5. The girl kissed the frog. Then, it turned into a handsome _____.
   ① prince ② prison ③ parent ④ pepper

6. The movie was _____. I recommend you see it.
   ① fat ② fantastic ③ friendly ④ full

7. Let's go to the beach. I bought a new _____ suit.
   ① sky ② ski ③ swim ④ swing

8. I'm in a skyscraper. The city view is just _____.
   ① awake ② amazing ③ aloud ④ afraid

9. Do you want to _____? You can join our club.
   ① do ② door ③ dance ④ dear

10. We're watching a modeling contest on TV. All the models are tall and _____.
    ① high ② hairy ③ hate ④ handsome

11. My sister is an actress. She is now _____ *Romeo and Juliet.*
    ① pushing ② performing ③ putting ④ pulling

12. Bob is the leader of his team. He has an important _____.
    ① red   ② role   ③ road   ④ rise

13. Who is your dance _____? Mine is Cathy.
    ① party   ② pants   ③ partner   ④ pancake

14. Pop singers are popular in Korea. _____ really like them.
    ① Trips   ② Tigers   ③ Tests   ④ Teenagers

15. I feel dizzy. I feel like the room is _____.
    ① spinning   ② stealing   ③ showing   ④ spreading

B 밑줄 친 단어와 비슷한 뜻을 가진 단어를 고르세요.

16. Hangeul is one of the <u>great</u> achievements of King Sejong.
    ① start   ② wonderful   ③ arrive   ④ stay

17. I was so <u>pleased</u> to hear of your success.
    ① grand   ② girlish   ③ gloomy   ④ glad

18. If you want to go to the bookstore, walk along this <u>street</u>.
    ① road   ② river   ③ round   ④ rope

C 밑줄 친 단어와 반대되는 뜻을 가진 단어를 고르세요.

19. Don't <u>pull</u> the door.
    ① peel   ② pain   ③ push   ④ pile

20. A bear <u>appeared</u> in the town.
    ① discounted   ② disappeared   ③ depressed   ④ did

Score: _____/20

Unit 3

Murphy's Law

Word Check

A 다음 단어들의 우리말 뜻을 모두 알고 있나요? 확인해 보세요.

> 단어의 품사에 맞는 우리말 뜻을 쓰세요.

1. ☐ law (명)
2. ☐ call (동)
3. ☐ example (명)
4. ☐ hour (명)
5. ☐ decide (동)
6. ☐ pass (동)
7. ☐ wallet (명)
8. ☐ school bag (명)
9. ☐ scold (동)
10. ☐ annoyed (형)
11. ☐ Coke (명)
12. ☐ problem (명)

13. ☐ wedding (명)
14. ☐ office (명)
15. ☐ wrong (형)
16. ☐ mechanic (명)
17. ☐ hurry (동)
18. ☐ miss (동)
19. ☐ suddenly (부)
20. ☐ reach (동)
21. ☐ barely (부)
22. ☐ balance (명)
23. ☐ fall on one's face (구)
24. ☐ unlucky (형)

B 우리말과 같은 뜻이 되도록 빈칸을 채워 영어 문장을 완성하세요.

1.	너는 머피의 법칙에 대해 알고 있니?	Do you know Murphy's 　　　　　　?
2.	잘못될 수 있는 어떤 일이 잘못되면 우리는 이것을 머피의 법칙이라고 부른다.	When anything that can go wrong does go wrong, we 　　　　　　 this Murphy's 　　　　　　.
3.	몇 가지 예를 들어보자.	Let me give you some 　　　　　　.

4.	너는 한 시간 동안 버스를 기다리는데 버스가 오지 않는다.	You wait for the bus for an _____, but it doesn't arrive.
5.	너는 택시를 타기로 결정한다.	You _____ to take a taxi.
6.	그런데 네가 택시를 타자마자 버스가 지나간다.	But as soon as you get in it, the bus _____ by.
7.	너는 지갑을 잃어버려서 새 것을 산다.	You lose your _____ and buy a new one.
8.	그런데 그것을 책가방 속에서 찾는다.	Then you find it in your _____.
9.	너의 엄마가 네가 하지 않은 일로 너를 꾸중하신다.	Your mom _____ you for something you didn't do.
10.	그래서 너는 짜증이 난다.	So you are _____.
11.	너는 콜라 캔을 찬다.	You kick a can of _____.
12.	그것이 경찰관의 머리에 맞아서 너는 곤란한 처지가 된다.	It hits a police officer's head and you have some _____.
13.	오늘은 루시의 고모의 결혼식이다.	Lucy's aunt has a _____ today.
14.	그녀의 아빠는 사무실에 가지 않는다.	Her father doesn't go to the _____.
15.	"차에 무슨 문제가 있는 거지?"	"What's _____ with the car?"
16.	"자동차 정비공을 불러야겠다."	"We should call a _____."
17.	"서둘러."	"_____ up."
18.	"그렇지 않으면 우리는 결혼식을 놓칠 거야!"	"Or we will _____ the wedding!"
19.	갑자기 어떤 차가 루시의 차를 친다.	_____, a car hits Lucy's car.
20.	그들은 결혼식에 가까스로 때맞추어 도착한다.	They _____ the wedding just in time.
21.	"우리는 간신히 도착했어. 어서 가자. 달려, 달려!"	"We _____ made it. Come on. Run, run!"
22.	루시는 그녀의 긴 드레스를 밟고 균형을 잃는다.	Lucy steps on her long dress and loses her _____.
23.	그녀는 앞으로 납작하게 넘어진다.	She _____ flat _____.
24.	"오, 이런! 정말 운이 나쁜 날이다!"	"Oh, my god! What an _____ day!"

A 빈칸에 어울리는 단어를 고르세요.

1. Someone _____ your name. Look out the window.
   ① catches ② calls ③ carries ④ costs

2. He fixed my car very well. He is a good _____.
   ① machine ② mechanic ③ maker ④ model

3. Let's take the math test. You have an _____.
   ① host ② house ③ hour ④ honor

4. We were so late. We _____ the train.
   ① minded ② missed ③ mistook ④ mixed

5. _____, I slipped on the floor. It was wet.
   ① Sweetly ② Strangely ③ Suddenly ④ Secretly

6. I have a big _____. It's very serious.
   ① produce ② problem ③ program ④ process

7. I _____ his house last night. He was in the garden.
   ① petted ② passed ③ put ④ posted

8. Fast food is not good for children. Here are some _____.
   ① enemies ② exits ③ exercises ④ examples

9. Don't break the _____. A police officer might catch you.
   ① lawn ② low ③ law ④ land

10. My dad is a businessman. He is in his _____.
    ① official ② counter ③ ocean ④ office

11. Today is my uncle's _____. I'm wearing a nice dress.
    ① pudding ② setting ③ dressing ④ wedding

12. I was late for school. The teacher _____ me.
    ① sold ② spent ③ scolded ④ suggested

13. If you _____ up, you can catch the bus.
    ① hurry   ② sorry   ③ worry   ④ curry

14. This is very difficult. I can _____ understand it.
    ① barely   ② barley   ③ rarely   ④ surely

15. I want to be a musician. So I _____ to go to music school.
    ① decide   ② develop   ③ describe   ④ design

B 밑줄 친 단어와 비슷한 뜻을 가진 단어를 고르세요.

16. Take an airplane. You will <u>reach</u> the city faster.
    ① arrive   ② leave   ③ bring   ④ ready

17. My brother always makes me feel <u>annoyed</u>. He is a little monster.
    ① confused   ② worried   ③ shy   ④ angry

18. I left my <u>wallet</u> at home. Can you lend me some money?
    ① coin   ② pocket   ③ purse   ④ bank

C 밑줄 친 단어와 반대되는 뜻을 가진 단어를 고르세요.

19. Today is Friday the 13th. People say it's an <u>unlucky</u> day.
    ① sticky   ② rocky   ③ lucky   ④ tricky

20. That's the <u>wrong</u> answer. Try to solve the problem again.
    ① strange   ② right   ③ light   ④ strong

Score: _____ /20

Mom's Words

Word Check

A 다음 단어들의 우리말 뜻을 모두 알고 있나요? 확인해 보세요.

> 단어의 품사에 맞는
> 우리말 뜻을 쓰세요.

1.	important	형	13.	nagging	명 형
2.	word	명	14.	oversleep	동
3.	future	명	15.	wash	동
4.	come true	구	16.	brush	동 명
5.	healthy	형	17.	comb	동 명
6.	regularly	부	18.	make a bed	구
7.	various	형	19.	chew	동
8.	challenge	동 명	20.	exercise	동 명
9.	honest	형	21.	read	동
10.	knock	동	22.	share	동
11.	hope	동 명	23.	wait	동
12.	postpone	동	24.	homework	명

B 우리말과 같은 뜻이 되도록 빈칸을 채워 영어 문장을 완성하세요.

1.	내가 너에게 중요한 몇 가지를 말할게.	I'll tell you something .
2.	제발 내 말을 들어라.	Please listen to my .
3.	나는 네가 너의 미래를 위해 큰 꿈을 가지기를 바란다.	I want you to have big dreams for your .

4.	나는 정말 네 꿈이 이루어지기를 바란다.	I really want your dreams to _____ _____.
5.	그리고 나는 네가 건강하기를 바란다.	And I want you to be _____.
6.	나는 네가 규칙적으로 운동하기를 바란다.	I want you to exercise _____.
7.	나는 네가 다양한 책들을 읽기를 바란다.	I want you to read _____ books.
8.	나는 네가 스스로 도전하기를 바란다.	I want you to _____ yourself.
9.	그리고 정직해라. 거짓말 하지 말아라.	And be _____. Don't tell lies.
10.	다른 사람의 방에 들어가기 전엔 문을 노크하렴.	_____ on the door before you enter another person's room.
11.	나는 정말로 네가 행복하게 살기를 바란다.	I really _____ that you live a happy life.
12.	제발 네가 해야 할 일을 뒤로 미루지 말아라.	Please don't _____ what you have to do.
13.	루시의 엄마가 루시에게 잔소리를 하고 있다.	Lucy's mom is _____ Lucy.
14.	"늦잠 자지 말아라."	"Don't _____."
15.	"세수해라."	"_____ your face."
16.	"양치질해라."	"_____ your teeth."
17.	"머리 빗어라."	"_____ your hair."
18.	"잠자리를 정돈해라."	"_____ your _____."
19.	"패스트푸드를 너무 많이 먹지 말아라. 천천히 씹어라."	"Don't eat too much fast food. _____ slowly."
20.	"건강해지기 위해 매일 운동해라."	"_____ every day to be healthy."
21.	"많은 책을 읽어라."	"_____ many books."
22.	"네 물건들을 친구들과 함께 써라."	"_____ your things with your friends."
23.	"네 순서를 기다려라."	"_____ your turn."
24.	"숙제해라."	"Do your _____."

A 빈칸에 어울리는 단어를 고르세요.

1. We eat _____ kinds of food every day.
   ① very   ② various   ③ happy   ④ ugly

2. Please _____ on your sister's door.
   ① knock   ② postpone   ③ hope   ④ visit

3. What do you want to be in the _____?
   ① yesterday   ② future   ③ today   ④ last month

4. I wanted to be a doctor and my dream _____ today.
   ① goes true   ② came true   ③ comes back   ④ goes back

5. It's _____ for children to listen to their parents.
   ① various   ② important   ③ hope   ④ postpone

6. Don't say bad _____. It's not nice.
   ① washes   ② walls   ③ waves   ④ words

7. My teacher asked me to _____ my book with a boy.
   ① share   ② oversleep   ③ homework   ④ wait

8. Every morning I _____ my hair.
   ① challenge   ② honest   ③ chew   ④ comb

9. He was late because he _____.
   ① overate   ② overcame   ③ overslept   ④ became

10. Please _____ your teeth before going to bed.
    ① wash   ② brush   ③ wipe   ④ exercise

11. Children don't like their parents' _____.
    ① nagging   ② brushing   ③ reading   ④ challenging

12. It's sunny. Let's _____ outside.
    ① regular   ② exercise   ③ chew   ④ hope

13. Why don't you _____ yourself?
   ① certain   ② confused   ③ contest   ④ challenge

14. Don't _____ gum in the classroom. Wrap and put it in the trash can.
   ① chew   ② check   ③ chilly   ④ cheer

15. Wake up! _____ and get dressed!
   ① Make money   ② Make food   ③ Make your bed   ④ Make a noise

B 밑줄 친 단어와 비슷한 뜻을 가진 단어를 고르세요.

16. We <u>postponed</u> our picnic because of the rain.
   ① put into   ② put down   ③ put on   ④ put off

17. I <u>hope</u> that I will become a famous person.
   ① wish   ② help   ③ wait   ④ wash

C 밑줄 친 단어와 반대되는 뜻을 가진 단어를 고르세요.

18. Try to eat <u>healthy</u> food like fruit and vegetables.
   ① unhappy   ② unhealthy   ③ unusual   ④ understand

19. Change your lifestyle. Try to eat <u>regularly</u>.
   ① irregularly   ② importantly   ③ nervous   ④ interesting

20. He is an <u>honest</u> boy. He never tells a lie.
   ① dislike   ② disappoint   ③ discover   ④ dishonest

Score: ____ /20

Bookworm

Word Check

A 다음 단어들의 우리말 뜻을 모두 알고 있나요? 확인해 보세요.

> 단어의 품사에 맞는
> 우리말 뜻을 쓰세요.

1.	award	명		13.	mirror	명	
2.	choose	동		14.	ask for	구	
3.	best	형	명	15.	become	동	
4.	check	동		16.	fan	명	
5.	vote	동		17.	wizard	명	
6.	fiction	명		18.	voice	명	
7.	some	형		19.	dark	명	형
8.	get	동		20.	dragon	명	
9.	bookmark	명		21.	rush	동	
10.	book report	명		22.	brave	형	
11.	bookworm	명		23.	spell	명	동
12.	right	부		24.	hold	동	

B 우리말과 같은 뜻이 되도록 빈칸을 채워 영어 문장을 완성하세요.

1.	어린이 도서 시상식 시간이 왔어요.	It's time for the Children's Book _____.
2.	학교 도서관에 가서 책을 고르세요.	Go to the school library and _____ a book.
3.	그것은 여러분이 가장 좋아하는 책이에요.	It's the book you like the _____.

4.	여러분이 가장 좋아하는 책을 확인하세요.	your favorite book.
5.	최고의 책에 투표를 하세요.	for the best book.
6.	픽션(허구) 제임스와 거대한 복숭아, 샬롯의 거미줄, 해리포터	– *James and the Giant Peach*, *Charlotte's Web*, *Harry Potter*
7.	또한 몇 가지 멋진 활동들이 있어요.	There are also _____ wonderful activities.
8.	여러분은 작가들을 만나고 사인을 받을 수 있어요.	You can meet writers and _____ autographs.
9.	여러분은 여러분만의 책갈피를 만들 수 있어요.	You can make your own _____.
10.	여러분은 친구들과 함께 독후감을 나눌 수 있어요.	You can share your _____ with your friends.
11.	그리고 나서 우리는 한 달에 10권 이상을 읽은 책벌레에게 상을 줄 거예요.	Then we'll give a prize to the _____ who reads over 10 books a month.
12.	지금 바로 오세요!	Please come _____ away!
13.	어느 날 밤, 흰 부엉이가 그녀의 거울에 나타난다.	One night, a white owl appears in her _____.
14.	루시는 부엉이에게 도움을 요청한다.	Lucy _____ the owl _____ help.
15.	루시는 해리를 만나서 흥분한다.	Lucy meets Harry, so she _____ excited.
16.	"나는 너의 최고의 팬이야."	"I'm your biggest _____."
17.	"어떻게 하면 내가 마법사가 될 수 있니?"	"How can I become a _____?"
18.	해리가 말한다:"쉿, 큰 소리로 말하지마. 날 따라와."	Harry says, "Shh, don't speak in a loud _____. Come with me."
19.	해리는 어둠 속에서 문을 연다.	Harry opens the door in the _____.
20.	용이 밤하늘을 날아간다.	A _____ is flying in the night sky.
21.	불이 용의 입 속으로 돌진한다.	A fire _____ into the dragon's mouth.
22.	루시가 말한다:"너는 매우 용감하구나."	Lucy says, "You are so _____."
23.	"나도 너의 주문을 배우고 싶어."	"I want to learn your _____."
24.	루시는 손에 주문 책을 쥔 채로 깨어난다.	Lucy wakes up _____ a spell book in her hand.

Review Test

 빈칸에 어울리는 단어를 고르세요.

1. Who will be the next leader? I will _____ for Alex.
   ① boat   ② volt   ③ both   ④ vote

2. I want to see a movie. Can I _____ a free ticket?
   ① eat   ② make   ③ set   ④ get

3. We have no time. Let's start _____ now.
   ① right   ② really   ③ wrist   ④ write

4. I like sweets. Can I have _____ candy bars?
   ① soon   ② some   ③ home   ④ room

5. Put your _____ in the book. Then you won't lose your place.
   ① book report   ② book cover   ③ bookmark   ④ bookcase

6. You're so loud. Keep your _____ down.
   ① prize   ② choice   ③ voice   ④ point

7. I came to _____ your help. Can I borrow your notebook?
   ① make for   ② ask for   ③ go out   ④ answer to

8. Here are green and blue ties. _____ one.
   ① Chew   ② Loose   ③ Shoot   ④ Choose

9. I like reading. My nickname is _____.
   ① yellow book   ② bookworm   ③ scrapbook   ④ comic book

10. Don't _____. You're not late.
    ① rush   ② crash   ③ lash   ④ lunch

11. Spring is nice and warm. Leaves _____ green.
    ① because   ② believe   ③ beside   ④ become

12. I didn't get the letter. I should _____ the mailbox.

   ① change   ② cheek   ③ check   ④ charm

13. I went to the Chinese festival. I saw a _____ dance.

   ① dragon   ② drama   ③ drawer   ④ develop

14. Look in the _____. You look nice in this green dress.

   ① middle   ② mirror   ③ error   ④ horror

15. Let's fix the roof. _____ the ladder, please.

   ① Hope   ② Hold   ③ Horn   ④ Hole

B 밑줄 친 단어와 비슷한 뜻을 가진 단어를 고르세요.

16. The best student wins an <u>award</u>. Do your best.

   ① goods   ② prize   ③ price   ④ gift

17. She told us the truth. She is <u>brave</u>.

   ① scared   ② smart   ③ courageous   ④ pleased

C 밑줄 친 단어와 반대되는 뜻을 가진 단어를 고르세요.

18. She can't sleep in the <u>dark</u>. I should wait until she falls asleep.

   ① backyard   ② light   ③ front   ④ along

19. This restaurant is the <u>best</u>. The food is so delicious.

   ① wrist   ② test   ③ vest   ④ worst

20. I like to read <u>fiction</u>. It's fun and exciting.

   ① nonstop   ② fictional   ③ nonfiction   ④ fearless

Score: _____ /20

About Cars

Word Check

A 다음 단어들의 우리말 뜻을 모두 알고 있나요? 확인해 보세요.

단어의 품사에 맞는 우리말 뜻을 쓰세요.

1.	quality	명	13.	road	명
2.	low	형	14.	traffic jam	명
3.	slogan	명	15.	severe	형
4.	produce	동	16.	stick	동 명
5.	system	명	17.	far	형
6.	mass	형	18.	get in[on]	구
7.	cheap	형	19.	shake	동
8.	price	명	20.	happen	동
9.	rich	형	21.	dizzy	형
10.	middle class	명	22.	airplane	명
11.	effect	명	23.	at last	구
12.	first	형	24.	really	부

B 우리말과 같은 뜻이 되도록 빈칸을 채워 영어 문장을 완성하세요.

1.	고품질	HIGH
2.	낮은 가격의 차	A _____ -PRICED CAR
3.	이것은 1909년 포드 자동차 모델 T의 포스터 표어였다.	This was the poster _____ of the Ford Model T in 1909.

4.	헨리 포드는 1908년부터 1927년까지 포드 모델 T를 생산했다.	Henry Ford _____ the Ford Model T from 1908 to 1927.
5.	포드는 조립라인이라는 새로운 방식으로 차를 만들었다.	Ford made the car with a new _____, the assembly line.
6.	포드 모델 T는 조립라인에서 대량으로 생산된 첫 번째 차였다.	The Ford Model T was the first car _____-produced on an assembly line.
7.	그 차는 무척 싸서 일반 사람들도 살 수 있었다.	It was so _____ that ordinary people could afford it.
8.	포드 모델 T가 나오기 전에는 자동차 가격들이 매우 비쌌다.	Before the Ford Model T, the _____ of cars were very expensive.
9.	그래서 오직 부자들만이 그 당시에 자동차를 살 수 있었다.	So only _____ people could buy cars at that time.
10.	그 자동차는 중산층의 미국 사람들이 쉽게 여행하는 것을 가능하게 해주었다.	The car made traveling easy for _____ Americans.
11.	포드는 사람들의 삶에 중요한 영향을 주었다.	Ford had an important _____ on people's lives.
12.	그것이 모델 T가 첫 번째 사람들의 자동차라고 불리는 이유이다.	That's why the Model T is called "the _____ people's car."
13.	많은 차들이 길 위에 있다.	Many cars are on the _____.
14.	"교통 체증이네."	"There's a _____."
15.	"심각하군."	"It's _____."
16.	"우리는 길 위에 갇혔어"라고 루시 아빠가 말한다.	"We're _____ on the road," says Lucy's dad.
17.	"우리는 집에서 너무 멀리 있어요."	"We're too _____ from home."
18.	루시와 아빠는 날아가는 차를 탄다.	Lucy and her dad _____ the flying car.
19.	그러나 날아가는 차가 흔들리기 시작한다.	However, the flying car begins to _____.
20.	"아빠, 무슨 일이에요?"	"Dad, what is _____?"
21.	"저 어지러워요."	"I feel _____."
22.	"루시야, 걱정 마. 비행기가 우리 옆을 지나갔어."	"Lucy, don't worry. An _____ flew past us."
23.	마침내 그들은 집에 도착한다.	_____, they arrive at home.
24.	"와! 집에 왔다. 그거 정말 빨랐어!"	"Wow! We're home. That was _____ fast!"

A 빈칸에 어울리는 단어를 고르세요.

1. It is not that expensive. It's _____.
   ① check   ② comic   ③ cheap   ④ chilly

2. Television is one of the most powerful forms of _____
   -media.
   ① mouse   ② mass   ③ mouth   ④ mess

3. Take the medicine after reading about the side-_____ of
   the medicine.
   ① effects   ② effort   ③ afraid   ④ affect

4. The _____ is down because the computer has an error.
   ① sister   ② sense   ③ system   ④ style

5. How much is it? I want to know the _____ of that
   notebook.
   ① prime   ② place   ③ praise   ④ price

6. The music is wonderful. I think it's _____ good.
   ① refer   ② really   ③ ready   ④ reader

7. Any volunteers? Who's going to do it _____?
   ① fit   ② face   ③ first   ④ family

8. If I want to go on the bus trip, I need to _____ the bus at
   9 o'clock.
   ① get on   ② gap   ③ gag   ④ got down

9. She traveled by _____.
   ① airport   ② airplane   ③ air bag   ④ airline

10. The storm is very _____. Many windows are broken.
    ① seven   ② serve   ③ save   ④ severe

11. Let's make a milkshake. Put vanilla ice cream into the milk and
    _____.
    ① shake ② shape ③ shock ④ shot

12. Wherever the trouble maker is, something _____.
    ① hopes ② happens ③ has ④ hangs

13. Don't spin your puppy around. He will feel _____.
    ① dirty ② difficult ③ cozy ④ dizzy

14. I am not low class or high class. I am just _____.
    ① class-mate ② mid-night ③ middle-aged ④ middle-class

15. If people throw trash in the river, the water _____ gets
    worse and worse.
    ① queen ② quality ③ quickly ④ qualify

Ⓑ 밑줄 친 단어와 비슷한 뜻을 가진 단어를 고르세요.

16. <u>At last</u>, my sister won a prize at the piano contest.
    ① Fully ② Finally ③ Finely ④ Finger

17. Follow this <u>road</u> for two blocks and turn right at the corner.
    ① straight ② sprit ③ street ④ screen

Ⓒ 밑줄 친 단어와 반대되는 뜻을 가진 단어를 고르세요.

18. Today's temperature is so <u>low</u>. I'm freeze.
    ① hi ② high ③ heat ④ hey

19. America is <u>far</u> from Korea. We have to take an airplane to get there.
    ① near ② nick ③ neck ④ new

20. I have a lot of money. I am a <u>rich</u> man.
    ① pure ② pork ③ pool ④ poor

Score: _____ /20

At the Beach

Word Check

Ⓐ 다음 단어들의 우리말 뜻을 모두 알고 있나요? 확인해 보세요.

> 단어의 품사에 맞는
> 우리말 뜻을 쓰세요.

1. ☐ beach	명		13. ☐ vacation	명	
2. ☐ view	명		14. ☐ get to	구	
3. ☐ relax	동		15. ☐ sea	명	
4. ☐ visitor	명		16. ☐ dive	동	
5. ☐ lie	동	명	17. ☐ breath	명	
6. ☐ along	부		18. ☐ glittering	형	
7. ☐ sell	동		19. ☐ deep	형	
8. ☐ fat	형		20. ☐ swallow	동	명
9. ☐ sandcastle	명		21. ☐ slippery	형	
10. ☐ water fight	명		22. ☐ inside	전	
11. ☐ shallow	형		23. ☐ spit	동	
12. ☐ surf	동		24. ☐ laugh	동	명

Ⓑ 우리말과 같은 뜻이 되도록 빈칸을 채워 영어 문장을 완성하세요.

1.	보라카이 해변은 필리핀에 있다.	Boracay _____ is in the Philippines.
2.	그 장소는 멋진 경치들로 유명하다.	The place is famous for its lovely _____.
3.	많은 사람들이 그곳에서 휴식을 취한다.	Many people _____ there.

4.	방문객들은 거기서 많은 것들을 즐길 수 있다.	_____ can enjoy many things there.
5.	여자가 태양 아래에 누워서 햇볕을 즐기고 있다.	A woman _____ in the sun and enjoys the sunshine.
6.	한 소녀가 길을 따라 걷는다.	A girl walks _____ the road.
7.	남자가 큰 파라솔 밑에서 아이스크림을 팔고 있다.	A man _____ ice cream under a large parasol.
8.	뚱뚱한 여자가 조개 껍질들을 찾는다.	A _____ woman searches for shells.
9.	소년이 모래성을 만든다.	A boy builds a _____.
10.	몇몇의 아이들은 물싸움을 한다.	Some kids have a _____.
11.	어린 꼬마들이 얕은 물에서 놀고 있다.	Little kids play in the _____ water.
12.	몇몇 사람들은 바다에서 파도타기를 한다.	Some people _____ the waves in the sea.
13.	루시의 가족이 해변으로 여름 휴가를 간다.	Lucy's family goes on a summer _____ to the beach.
14.	그녀의 아빠가 운전해서 해변에 도착한다.	Her dad drives to _____ the beach.
15.	루시는 바다 밑을 탐험하고 싶다.	Lucy wants to explore under the _____.
16.	그녀는 물안경을 쓰고 바다로 잠수한다.	She wears goggles and _____ into the sea.
17.	그녀는 물속에서 숨을 참는다.	She holds her _____ underwater.
18.	"화려한 물고기들을 봐. 반짝거려."	"Look at the colorful fish. They are _____."
19.	그녀는 바다 속으로 더 깊이 수영한다.	She swims _____ into the sea.
20.	돌고래 한 마리가 큰 입으로 루시를 삼킨다.	A dolphin _____ Lucy in its big mouth.
21.	"정말 어둡고 미끄럽네."	"It's really dark and _____."
22.	그녀는 돌고래 안에 있다.	She is _____ the dolphin.
23.	돌고래가 그녀를 뱉는다.	The dolphin _____ her out.
24.	미스터 돌고래가 웃는다.	Mr. Dolphin _____.

A 빈칸에 어울리는 단어를 고르세요.

1. I don't like being _____. I want to lose weight.
   ① fast   ② flat   ③ fat   ④ fresh

2. You need to _____. Make yourself at home.
   ① reach   ② relax   ③ record   ④ regret

3. Sam is collecting seashells. Linda is building a sandcastle at the _____.
   ① bicycle   ② bottle   ③ bricks   ④ beach

4. I'm so tired. I want to _____ on the bed.
   ① like   ② live   ③ lie   ④ lose

5. Swim in _____ water. It's dangerous to swim in deep water.
   ① shallow   ② swallow   ③ swing   ④ sweet

6. Look at that cool guy. He is _____ the waves.
   ① supporting   ② surfing   ③ suffering   ④ studying

7. Lots of living things like seaweed and fish are under the _____.
   ① soil   ② skirt   ③ sea   ④ snack

8. They _____ notebooks, pencils, and glue at the stationary store.
   ① sail   ② sell   ③ say   ④ spell

9. I'm late. I should _____ the bus station on time.
   ① get ready   ② get tired   ③ get some rest   ④ get to

10. A frog jumps out of the grass. Suddenly a snake _____ it in its mouth.
    ① swims   ② switches   ③ surprises   ④ swallows

11. This floor is _____. Be careful not to slip on the floor.
    ① slippery   ② spin   ③ secret   ④ sleepy

12. I dived into the _____ blue sea to look at the beautiful sea creatures.
    ① date   ② deep   ③ dear   ④ dirty

13. It's a jewelry box. Those _____ things are diamonds.
    ① glad   ② gather   ③ green   ④ glittering

14. Close your eyes. Then take a deep _____ in and out.
    ① break   ② breath   ③ bring   ④ branch

15. Don't _____ gum on the street. Put it in the trash can.
    ① spit   ② speak   ③ shout   ④ spread

B 밑줄 친 단어와 비슷한 뜻을 가진 단어를 고르세요.

16. I get to school at 8:30 in the morning.
    ① start   ② leave   ③ arrive   ④ stay

17. He's so funny. His jokes make me laugh.
    ① cry   ② giggle   ③ thirsty   ④ slippery

18. I traveled to Paris with my family. The view from the Effel Tower was wonderful.
    ① ocean   ② slip   ③ scene   ④ taste

C 밑줄 친 단어와 반대되는 뜻을 가진 단어를 고르세요.

19. I'm playing inside the house.
    ① backyard   ② outside   ③ front   ④ along

20. This swimming pool is shallow. So it's safe to swim here.
    ① sharp   ② small   ③ large   ④ deep

Score: _____/20

I Enjoy Cooking

Word Check

A 다음 단어들의 우리말 뜻을 모두 알고 있나요? 확인해 보세요.

> 단어의 품사에 맞는 우리말 뜻을 쓰세요.

1. ☐ health ⒨
2. ☐ ingredient ⒨
3. ☐ oil ⒨
4. ☐ onion ⒨
5. ☐ carrot ⒨
6. ☐ potato ⒨
7. ☐ chicken ⒨
8. ☐ how to+동사원형 ⒢
9. ☐ peel ⒟ ⒨
10. ☐ fry ⒟
11. ☐ add ⒟
12. ☐ minute ⒨

13. ☐ topic ⒨
14. ☐ chef ⒨
15. ☐ well ⒝
16. ☐ happy ⒣
17. ☐ fridge ⒨
18. ☐ egg ⒨
19. ☐ enough ⒣
20. ☐ tooth ⒨
21. ☐ hen ⒨
22. ☐ pot ⒨
23. ☐ mix ⒟
24. ☐ simmer ⒟

B 우리말과 같은 뜻이 되도록 빈칸을 채워 영어 문장을 완성하세요.

1.	카레는 우리의 건강에 좋다.	Curry is good for our _____.
2.	재료들	
3.	기름	

4.	양파 한 개	one
5.	당근 한 개	one
6.	감자 두 개	two
7.	닭고기 400 그램	400 g
8.	만드는 법	Make
9.	첫째, 채소들의 껍질을 벗겨라.	First, the vegetables.
10.	셋째, 그것들을 팬에 넣고 기름에 볶아라.	Third, put them in a pan and them in oil.
11.	마지막으로, 카레 가루와 물을 추가해라.	Finally, the curry powder and water.
12.	40분 동안 요리한다.	Cook for 40 .
13.	그 회의의 주제가 뭔가요?	What's the main for the meeting?
14.	미스터 쿡은 훌륭한 주방장이다.	Mr. Cook is a great .
15.	그는 요리를 매우 잘한다.	He cooks very .
16.	그들은 가장 행복한 음식을 만들기 위해 재료들을 준비한다.	They prepare some ingredients for the meal.
17.	루시는 재료를 얻기 위해 냉장고 안을 살펴본다.	Lucy looks in the to get some ingredients.
18.	그녀는 달걀 한 개와 채소들을 좀 꺼낸다.	She takes out one and some vegetables.
19.	미스터 쿡이 말한다. "이것으론 충분하지 않아. 우린 뭔가 더 필요해."	Mr. Cook says, "It's not . We need something more."
20.	그는 금붕어의 이빨과 암탉의 발을 좀 가져온다.	He gets a goldfish's and some 's feet.
21.	그들은 그것들을 냄비에 담는다.	They put them in the .
22.	"그것들을 함께 섞자." 미스터 쿡이 말한다.	"Let's them together," says Mr. Cook.
23.	"그것들을 끓여요." 루시가 말한다.	"Let's them," says Lucy.

Review Test

 빈칸에 어울리는 단어를 고르세요.

1. I'll give you three _____ . Please finish your homework.
   ① well   ② fry   ③ minutes   ④ peel

2. A _____ is a root vegetable. It's orange and long.
   ① potato   ② onion   ③ carrot   ④ pepper

3. _____ and wash the potatoes before cooking them.
   ① Fry   ② Peel   ③ Mix   ④ Ingredient

4. When I peel an _____ , it makes my eyes water.
   ① carrot   ② onion   ③ potato   ④ sweet potato

5. Could you teach me _____ make chicken curry?
   ① how to   ② how good   ③ where to   ④ what to

6. When I cook spaghetti, I use a lot of _____ .
   ① teeth   ② fridge   ③ simmer   ④ ingredients

7. I have _____ food in the fridge.
   ① enough   ② egg   ③ well   ④ pot

8. A shark's _____ is sharp.
   ① mouth   ② hair   ③ tooth   ④ potato

9. When you are sick, _____ soup makes you feel better.
   ① chalk   ② clay   ③ chicken   ④ chest

10. The _____ is to write about yesterday's weather.
    ① hen   ② topic   ③ carrot   ④ study

11. The boy _____ the red and white paint together.
    ① mixes   ② hurries   ③ appears   ④ cooks

12. Do you like pork cutlet? Let's _____ the cutlets in oil.
    ① wash   ② well   ③ minute   ④ fry

13. Pour some water into the _____. They do not mix.
   ① juice   ② oil   ③ Coke   ④ soda

14. A chicken lays an _____. A chick comes out of it.
   ① baby   ② egg   ③ young   ④ adult

15. Take a _____ and fill it with water. Put it on the stove and heat it.
   ① plate   ② dish   ③ spoon   ④ pot

B 밑줄 친 단어와 비슷한 뜻을 가진 단어를 고르세요.

16. When my mother makes chicken soup, she <u>simmers</u> it for two hours.
   ① mixes   ② cuts   ③ boils   ④ bothers

17. The <u>chef</u> of this restaurant is really good. He cooks very delicious food.
   ① cook   ② waitress   ③ owner   ④ cleaner

C 밑줄 친 단어와 반대되는 뜻을 가진 단어를 고르세요.

18. I had a <u>happy</u> time with my family.
   ① excited   ② alive   ③ impossible   ④ unhappy

19. A <u>hen</u> is pecking at the feed with its beak.
   ① gull   ② parrot   ③ rooster   ④ swallow

20. Please <u>add</u> some sugar to my hot chocolate.
   ② allow   ② subtract   ③ shake   ④ pull

Score: _____/20

Unit 9

At the Hospital

Word Check

A 다음 단어들의 우리말 뜻을 모두 알고 있나요? 확인해 보세요.

> 단어의 품사에 맞는 우리말 뜻을 쓰세요.

1. ☐ hospital (명)	13. ☐ be able to (구)
2. ☐ emergency (형) (명)	14. ☐ instead of (구)
3. ☐ crowded (형)	15. ☐ disguise (동)
4. ☐ headache (명)	16. ☐ clinic (명)
5. ☐ worry (동)	17. ☐ ill (형)
6. ☐ bleed (동)	18. ☐ pretend (동)
7. ☐ bandage (명)	19. ☐ stomachache (명)
8. ☐ hurt (동)	20. ☐ prescribe (동)
9. ☐ stay (동)	21. ☐ fall in love (구)
10. ☐ patient (명)	22. ☐ give a shot (구)
11. ☐ symptom (명)	23. ☐ take a rest (구)
12. ☐ treat (동)	24. ☐ excellent (형)

B 우리말과 같은 뜻이 되도록 빈칸을 채워 영어 문장을 완성하세요.

1.	아픈 사람들은 병원에 간다.	Sick people go to the _____.
2.	응급실은 하루 종일 붐빈다.	The _____ room is busy all day.
3.	그곳은 병원에서 가장 혼잡한 장소이다.	It is the most _____ place in the hospital.

4.	머리가 아픈 소년이 울고 있다.	A boy who has a is crying.
5.	그의 엄마는 그를 걱정한다.	His mother about him.
6.	피를 흘리는 남자가 앰뷸런스에서 들것에 실려 온다.	A man is carried in on a stretcher from the ambulance.
7.	그는 팔을 다쳤다.	He his arm.
8.	간호사가 그의 팔에 붕대를 감아준다.	A nurse puts a on his arm.
9.	의사들과 간호사들은 하루 종일 그곳에 머무른다.	Doctors and nurses there all day.
10.	그들은 환자들을 돌보느라 항상 바쁘다.	They are always busy taking care of .
11.	아픈 사람들은 다른 종류의 증상들을 갖고 있다.	Sick people have different kinds of .
12.	의사와 간호사는 다른 방법들로 그들을 치료한다.	Doctors and nurses them in different ways.
13.	루시의 아빠는 아파서 일을 하러 갈 수 없었다.	Lucy's father got sick and wasn't to go to work.
14.	루시는 아빠 대신에 일하러 가기로 결심했다.	Lucy decided to go to work her father.
15.	그녀는 의사로 변장했다.	She herself as a doctor.
16.	한 소년이 엄마와 함께 개인병원에 왔다.	A boy came to the with his mother.
17.	그는 아파 보이지만 사실은 아니다.	He looks but actually he isn't.
18.	그는 학교에 가기 싫어서 아픈 척했다.	He to be ill because he didn't want to go to school.
19.	"배가 아파요"라고 소년이 말했다.	"I have a ," said the boy.
20.	루시는 소년에게 가짜 약을 좀 처방했다.	Lucy the boy some fake medicine.
21.	다음 환자는 사랑에 빠진 남자였다.	The next patient was a man who .
22.	루시는 한 여자에게 주사를 놓아 주었는데, 그러자 그녀의 기분이 나아졌다.	Lucy a woman , which made her feel better.
23.	루시는 또한 그녀에게 휴식을 취하라고 말했다.	Lucy also told her to .
24.	그녀는 의사로서 훌륭하게 잘 해냈다.	She did an job as a doctor.

A 빈칸에 어울리는 단어를 고르세요.

1. I fell down on the ground. My leg _____ a lot.
   ① hates   ② hurts   ③ hires   ④ happens

2. Will you _____ with me? I'm scared.
   ① reach   ② stop   ③ stay   ④ regret

3. Don't _____ about me. I'll be fine.
   ① work   ② want   ③ win   ④ worry

4. I have a _____. I need to see a doctor.
   ① head   ② headache   ③ horse   ④ hand

5. I heard that Janet is in the _____. Let's visit her.
   ① hospital   ② honey   ③ hiking   ④ hope

6. It's Children's Day. The amusement park is so _____.
   ① certain   ② central   ③ clean   ④ crowded

7. She cut her finger. It's _____.
   ① baking   ② bending   ③ bleeding   ④ bedding

8. Ben has his arm in _____. He hurt his arm.
   ① bridges   ② bakers   ③ bandages   ④ brides

9. Scott is at a clinic. He tells his _____ to the doctor.
   ① states   ② sands   ③ songs   ④ symptoms

10. Does this hospital have an _____ room? My daughter is very sick.
    ① elephant   ② emergency   ③ earrings   ④ excellence

11. It's Halloween. Owen _____ himself as a vampire.
    ① disguises   ② does   ③ drops   ④ diets

12. The doctor gave me a _____. I feel better now.
    ① shop   ② ship   ③ shot   ④ show

13. I have a _____. I guess it's because I ate something bad.
    ① spring   ② screen   ③ store   ④ stomachache

14. The doctor _____ me painkillers. I can get them at the drug store.
    ① printed   ② prescribed   ③ prided   ④ peeled

15. He _____ in love at first sight. But it's one-sided.
    ① fell   ② filled   ③ found   ④ followed

밑줄 친 단어와 비슷한 뜻을 가진 단어를 고르세요.

16. My dog was seriously ill.
    ① spin   ② sick   ③ strong   ④ sink

17. John is an excellent player on our team.
    ① gain   ② good   ③ get   ④ great

18. Karan is able to ride a bike by herself.
    ① can't   ② could   ③ can   ④ care

19. You should take a rest at home.
    ① take a break ② take a bath ③ take a picture ④ take a medicine

C 밑줄 친 단어와 반대되는 뜻을 가진 단어를 고르세요.

20. The patient is getting better.
    ① doctor   ② dear   ③ dream   ④ dad

Score: _____ /20

Unit 9 | At the Hospital 37

Roller Coaster

Word Check

A 다음 단어들의 우리말 뜻을 모두 알고 있나요? 확인해 보세요.

> 단어의 품사에 맞는 우리말 뜻을 쓰세요.

1. ☐ guess	동 명	13. ☐ yesterday	명
2. ☐ because	접	14. ☐ thirsty	형
3. ☐ top	명	15. ☐ buy	동
4. ☐ rider	명	16. ☐ imagine	동
5. ☐ while	접	17. ☐ lamp	명
6. ☐ which	대 형	18. ☐ seat	명
7. ☐ rapidly	부	19. ☐ steal	동
8. ☐ increase	동	20. ☐ maze	명
9. ☐ thrill	명 동	21. ☐ escape	동 명
10. ☐ fear	명 동	22. ☐ gate	명
11. ☐ at the same time	구	23. ☐ moment	명
12. ☐ located	형	24. ☐ adventure	명

B 우리말과 같은 뜻이 되도록 빈칸을 채워 영어 문장을 완성하세요.

1.	당신은 그 이유를 추측할 수 있는가?	Can you _____ the reason?
2.	그것은 속도가 사람들을 흥분시키기 때문이다.	It's _____ the speed makes people excited.
3.	롤러 코스터는 꼭대기까지 천천히 간다.	Roller coasters go slowly to the _____.

4.	탑승자들은 흥분하고 긴장한다.	The _____ feel excited and nervous.
5.	그들은 그것이 꼭대기까지 올라가는 동안 흥분하고 긴장한다.	They feel excited and nervous _____ it's going up to the top.
6.	꼭대기에 도달한 롤러 코스터는 하강한다.	The roller coaster _____ reaches the top goes down.
7.	그것은 급격하게 떨어진다.	It goes down _____ .
8.	롤러 코스터의 속도가 증가한다.	The speed of the roller coaster _____ .
9.	갑작스런 속도의 변화는 사람들이 전율을 느끼게 한다.	A sudden change in speed makes people get a _____ .
10.	또한 그들은 공포를 느낀다.	Also they feel _____ .
11.	그들은 동시에 두 가지 감정을 경험한다.	They experience two feelings _____ .
12.	가장 빠른 롤러 코스터는 아랍 에미레이트 공화국에 있는 페라리 월드에 위치한 포뮬라 로사이다.	The fastest roller coaster is Formula Rossa, _____ at Ferrari World in the United Arab Emirates.
13.	루시는 어제 놀이동산에 갔다.	Lucy went to the amusement park _____ .
14.	루시는 목이 말랐다.	Lucy felt _____ .
15.	그래서 루시는 물 한 병을 사서 마셨다.	So Lucy _____ a bottle of water and drank it.
16.	'이 물을 마시면 당신이 상상한 것을 얻을 수 있다.' 라고 물병에 쓰여 있었다.	"You can get what you _____ if you drink this," was written on the bottle.
17.	루시는 알라딘의 요술 램프를 생각했다.	Lucy thought about Aladdin's magic _____ .
18.	뒷좌석에 마법사가 나타났다.	A wizard appeared in the back _____ .
19.	그는 그 램프를 훔치려고 했다.	He tried to _____ the lamp.
20.	루시와 지니는 미로로 갔다.	Lucy and the genie went into the _____ .
21.	하지만 루시는 미로에서 탈출하고 싶었다.	But Lucy wanted to _____ from the maze.
22.	"지니, 제발 출구를 찾아 줘."루시가 말했다.	"Find the _____ , please, Genie," said Lucy.
23.	그 순간 루시는 출입문 밖에 나타났다.	At that _____ , Lucy appeared on the outside of the gate.
24.	루시는 집에 가서 가족에게 지니와 함께한 모험에 대해 말해주었다.	Lucy went home and told her family about her _____ with the genie.

A 빈칸에 어울리는 단어를 고르세요.

1. Close your eyes and _____ your future girlfriend.
   ① imagine   ② image   ③ interest   ④ steal

2. I like summer _____ I can go swimming outdoors.
   ① but   ② because   ③ which   ④ when

3. Where is the main _____? He is waiting for me there.
   ① dish   ② price   ③ gate   ④ dessert

4. I lost my watch. Somebody might have _____ it.
   ① spit   ② escape   ③ stolen   ④ moment

5. The city is dangerous. One lion _____ from the zoo.
   ① ate   ② explored   ③ mixed   ④ escaped

6. Wait a _____. I'll finish soon. Then, let's go out together.
   ① moment   ② meal   ③ mirror   ④ medicine

7. Yellowstone National Park is _____ in the USA.
   ① adventure   ② located   ③ limited   ④ maze

8. I am _____. Can I have some water, please?
   ① thirsty   ② happy   ③ sad   ④ interested

9. Surprise! Can you _____ what your birthday present is?
   ① jump   ② guess   ③ add   ④ buy

10. My sister sits on my _____.
    ① seat   ② breaths   ③ fear   ④ rider

11. I was excited _____ I watched the movie.
    ① with   ② under   ③ how   ④ while

12. I went to the park _____. I rode a bike with my friend.
    ① vacation   ② yesterday   ③ tomorrow   ④ in the future

13. Let's go on an _____ to an unknown world. Follow me!
　　① advertise　　② address　　③ adventure　　④ arrival

14. Get out of the _____. If you get out first, you will be the winner.
　　① puzzle　　② riddle　　③ quiz　　④ maze

15. It gave me a _____ that somebody called my name. I was the winner.
　　① fear　　② thrill　　③ anger　　④ disappointment

B 밑줄 친 단어와 비슷한 뜻을 가진 단어를 고르세요.

16. Hiking is good for your health. Let's climb to the <u>top</u> of the mountain.
　　① peak　　② picky　　③ part　　④ pile

17. When I went to the haunted house, I felt a lot of <u>fear</u>.
　　① exciting　　② dramatic　　③ horror　　④ fantastic

18. I can listen to music and read a book <u>at the same time</u>.
　　① at the same point　　② at the same moment
　　③ at the same house　　④ at the different moment

C 밑줄 친 단어와 반대되는 뜻을 가진 단어를 고르세요.

19. I will <u>buy</u> a ticket for the movie. I really like that movie a lot.
　　① fold　　② sell　　③ get　　④ borrow

20. The number of cars is <u>increasing</u> in the city.
　　① speeding　　② destroying　　③ decreasing　　④ selling

Score: _____ /20

• Answers •

Unit 1 My Collection p.2

Word Check

Ⓐ 1. 돈 2. ~할 때; 언제 3. 세계, 세상
4. 수집하다, 모으다 5. 지도 6. 동전 7. 얼굴
8. 나타내다, 상징하다 9. 지폐 10. 스크랩북
11. 구겨지다, 주름이 지다 12. 기억, 추억
13. ~와 함께 14. 항상, 언제나 15. 낮잠
16. 껴안다, 포옹하다 17. 구름이 낀, 흐린
18. 빛, 조명; 밝은 19. 어디에; ~한 곳에
20. 대회, 시합 21. 살아 있는 22. 무대 23. 상
24. 자랑스러운

Ⓑ 1. money 2. when 3. world 4. collect
5. map 6. coins 7. faces 8. represent 9. Bills
10. scrapbook 11. wrinkled 12. memories
13. with 14. always 15. nap 16. hugging
17. cloudy 18. light 19. where 20. contest
21. alive 22. stage 23. prize 24. proud

Review Test

Ⓐ 1. ① 2. ③ 3. ④ 4. ③ 5. ① 6. ② 7. ②
8. ④ 9. ③ 10. ① 11. ③ 12. ④ 13. ②
14. ① 15. ①

Ⓑ 16. ② 17. ② 18. ① 19. ④

Ⓒ 20. ③

Unit 2 Amazing B-Boy Dancers p.6

Word Check

Ⓐ 1. 춤추다; 춤 2. 십대 3. 놀라운 4. 회전하다, 돌다
5. 속도 6. 또 하나의, 다른 7. 지지하다, 떠받치다
8. 박수를 치다 9. 열심히; 어려운 10. 모든, 매 ~마다
11. 대단한, 훌륭한 12. 기쁜 13. 공연하다 14. 역할
15. 동반자, 파트너 16. 길, 거리 17. 잘생긴
18. 당기다 19. 환상적인 20. 왕자 21. 수영하다
22. 나타나다 23. 무릎을 꿇다 24. 함께, 같이

Ⓑ 1. dances 2. teenagers 3. amazing 4. spins
5. speeds 6. another 7. supports
8. give, a big hand 9. hard 10. Every 11. great
12. pleased 13. perform 14. role 15. partner
16. street 17. handsome 18. pulls
19. fantastic 20. prince 21. swims 22. appears
23. goes down on one knee 24. together

Review Test

Ⓐ 1. ③ 2. ② 3. ④ 4. ③ 5. ① 6. ② 7. ③
8. ② 9. ③ 10. ④ 11. ② 12. ② 13. ③
14. ④ 15. ①

Ⓑ 16. ② 17. ④ 18. ①

Ⓒ 19. ③ 20. ②

Unit 3 Murphy's Law p.10

Word Check

Ⓐ 1. 법 2. 부르다 3. 예, 본보기 4. 시간 5. 결정하다
6. 지나가다 7. 지갑 8. 책가방 9. 혼내다
10. 짜증 나는, 화가 난 11. 콜라 12. 문제
13. 결혼(식) 14. 사무실, 회사 15. 틀린 16. 정비공
17. 서두르다 18. 놓치다 19. 갑자기 20. 도착하다
21. 간신히 22. 균형 23. 앞으로 넘어지다
24. 운이 없는

Ⓑ 1. Law 2. call, Law 3. examples 4. hour
5. decide 6. passes 7. wallet 8. school bag
9. scolds 10. annoyed 11. Coke 12. problems
13. wedding 14. office 15. wrong
16. mechanic 17. Hurry 18. miss 19. Suddenly
20. reach 21. barely 22. balance
23. falls, on her face 24. unlucky

Review Test

Ⓐ 1. ② 2. ② 3. ③ 4. ② 5. ③ 6. ② 7. ②
8. ④ 9. ③ 10. ④ 11. ④ 12. ③ 13. ①
14. ① 15. ①

Ⓑ 16. ① 17. ④ 18. ③

Ⓒ 19. ③ 20. ②

Unit 4 Mom's Words p.14

| Word Check |

Ⓐ 1. 중요한 2. 말, 낱말, 단어 3. 미래 4. 실현되다
5. 건강한, 건강에 좋은 6. 규칙적으로 7. 다양한
8. 시도하다; 도전 9. 정직한 10. (문을) 두드리다
11. 바라다; 희망 12. 뒤로 미루다
13. 잔소리; 잔소리가 심한 14. 늦잠 자다 15. 씻다
16. (솔로) 닦다; 솔 17. 빗질하다; 머리빗
18. 잠자리를 정돈하다 19. 씹다 20. 운동하다; 운동
21. 읽다 22. 함께 쓰다 23. 기다리다 24. 숙제

Ⓑ 1. important 2. words 3. future 4. come true
5. healthy 6. regularly 7. various 8. challenge
9. honest 10. Knock 11. hope 12. postpone
13. nagging 14. oversleep 15. Wash
16. Brush 17. Comb 18. Make, bed 19. Chew
20. Exercise 21. Read 22. Share 23. Wait
24. homework

| Review Test |

Ⓐ 1. ② 2. ① 3. ② 4. ② 5. ② 6. ④ 7. ①
8. ④ 9. ③ 10. ② 11. ① 12. ② 13. ④
14. ① 15. ③

Ⓑ 16. ④ 17. ①

Ⓒ 18. ② 19. ① 20. ④

Unit 5 Bookworm p.18

| Word Check |

Ⓐ 1. 상 2. 선택하다 3. 가장 좋은; 최고 4. 확인하다
5. 투표하다 6. 소설, 꾸며낸 이야기
7. 약간의, 얼마간의 8. 받다, 얻다 9. 책갈피
10. 독후감, 독서 감상문 11. 책벌레, 독서광
12. 곧장, 곧바로 13. 거울
14. ~을 요청하다, ~을 부탁하다 15. ~이 되다
16. 팬 17. 마법사 18. 목소리 19. 어둠; 어두운
20. 용 21. 돌진하다 22. 용감한
23. 주문; 주문을 외우다 24. 잡다

Ⓑ 1. Awards 2. choose 3. best 4. Check
5. Vote 6. Fiction 7. some 8. get
9. bookmark 10. book report 11. bookworm

12. right 13. mirror 14. asks, for 15. becomes
16. fan 17. wizard 18. voice 19. dark
20. dragon 21. rushes 22. brave 23. spell
24. holding

| Review Test |

Ⓐ 1. ④ 2. ④ 3. ① 4. ② 5. ③ 6. ③ 7. ②
8. ④ 9. ② 10. ① 11. ④ 12. ③ 13. ①
14. ② 15. ②

Ⓑ 16. ② 17. ③

Ⓒ 18. ② 19. ④ 20. ③

Unit 6 About Cars p.22

| Word Check |

Ⓐ 1. 질 2. 낮은 3. 표어 4. 제작하다, 만들다
5. 방식, 시스템 6. 대중의, 많은 양의 7. 싼 8. 가격
9. 부자인 10. 중간 계층, 중산층 11. 영향, 효과
12. 처음의 13. 길 14. 교통혼잡 15. 엄한, 심한
16. 끼어들게 하다, 꼼짝 못하다; 막대기
17. (거리가) 먼 18. (차를) 타다 19. 흔들다
20. (사건이) 일어나다 21. 어지러운 22. 비행기
23. 마침내 24. 정말, 진짜

Ⓑ 1. QUALITY 2. LOW 3. slogan 4. produced
5. system 6. mass 7. cheap 8. prices 9. rich
10. middle class 11. effect 12. first 13. road
14. traffic jam 15. severe 16. stuck 17. far
18. get in 19. shake 20. happening 21. dizzy
22. airplane 23. At last 24. really

| Review Test |

Ⓐ 1. ③ 2. ② 3. ① 4. ③ 5. ④ 6. ② 7. ③
8. ① 9. ② 10. ④ 11. ① 12. ② 13. ④
14. ④ 15. ②

Ⓑ 16. ② 17. ③

Ⓒ 18. ② 19. ① 20. ④

Word Check

Ⓐ 1. 해변   2. 경치, 경관   3. 휴식을 취하다
4. 손님, 방문객   5. 눕다, 거짓말하다; 거짓말
6. ~을 따라서   7. 팔다   8. 뚱뚱한   9. 모래성
10. 물싸움   11. 얕은   12. 파도타기를 하다
13. 방학, 휴가   14. 도착하다   15. 바다
16. 잠수하다, (물속으로) 뛰어들다   17. 숨
18. 반짝이는, 빛나는   19. 깊은   20. 삼키다; 제비
21. 미끄러운   22. ~의 안에   23. 뱉다, 토하다
24. 웃다; 웃음

Ⓑ 1. Beach   2. views   3. relax   4. Visitors   5. lies
6. along   7. sells   8. fat   9. sandcastle
10. water fight   11. shallow   12. surf
13. vacation   14. get to   15. sea   16. dives
17. breath   18. glittering   19. deeper
20. swallows   21. slippery   22. inside   23. spits
24. laughs

Review Test

Ⓐ 1. ③   2. ②   3. ④   4. ③   5. ①   6. ②   7. ③
8. ②   9. ④   10. ④   11. ①   12. ②   13. ④
14. ②   15. ①

Ⓑ 16. ③   17. ②   18. ③

Ⓒ 19. ②   20. ④

Word Check

Ⓐ 1. 건강   2. 재료, 원료   3. 기름   4. 양파   5. 당근
6. 감자   7. 닭, 닭고기   8. ~하는 방법
9. 껍질을 벗기다; 껍질   10. (기름에) 볶다, 튀기다
11. 더하다, 추가하다   12. 분, 순간   13. 주제
14. 주방장   15. 잘   16. 행복한   17. 냉장고   18. 달걀
19. 충분한   20. 이, 치아   21. 암탉   22. 냄비
23. 섞다, 혼합하다   24. 끓이다

Ⓑ 1. health   2. Ingredients   3. oil   4. onion
5. carrot   6. potatoes   7. chicken   8. How to
9. peel   10. fry   11. add   12. minutes   13. topic
14. chef   15. well   16. happiest   17. fridge
18. egg   19. enough   20. tooth, hen   21. pot
22. mix   23. simmer

Review Test

Ⓐ 1. ③   2. ③   3. ②   4. ②   5. ①   6. ④   7. ①
8. ③   9. ③   10. ②   11. ①   12. ④   13. ②
14. ②   15. ④

Ⓑ 16. ③   17. ①

Ⓒ 18. ④   19. ③   20. ②

Word Check

Ⓐ 1. 병원   2. 긴급한; 위급, 비상   3. 붐비는, 복잡한
4. 두통   5. 걱정하다   6. 피가 나다   7. 붕대
8. 다치게 하다, 아프다   9. 머무르다   10. 환자
11. 증상   12. 치료하다, 처치하다   13. ~할 수 있다
14. ~ 대신에   15. 변장시키다, 속이다   16. 개인병원
17. 아픈   18. ~인 체하다   19. 복통   20. 처방하다
21. 사랑에 빠지다   22. 주사를 놓다   23. 쉬다
24. 훌륭한

Ⓑ 1. hospital   2. emergency   3. crowded
4. headache   5. worries   6. bleeding
7. hurt   8. bandage   9. stay   10. patients
11. symptoms   12. treat   13. able   14. instead of
15. disguised   16. clinic   17. ill   18. pretended
19. stomachache   20. prescribed   21. fell in love
22. gave, a shot   23. take a rest   24. excellent

Review Test

Ⓐ 1. ②   2. ③   3. ④   4. ②   5. ①   6. ④   7. ③
8. ③   9. ④   10. ②   11. ①   12. ③   13. ④
14. ②   15. ①

Ⓑ 16. ②   17. ④   18. ③   19. ①

Ⓒ 20. ①

Unit 10 Roller Coaster　　p.38

| Word Check |

A
1. 추측하다; 추측　2. ~ 때문에　3. 꼭대기
4. 타는 사람　5. ~ 동안　6. 어느 것; 어느
7. 빠르게, 급격하게　8. 증가하다
9. 전율, 흥분, 설렘; 열광시키다, 감동시키다
10. 공포; 무서워하다　11. 동시에, 잠깐, 잠시
12. ~에 위치한　13. 어제　14. 목마른　15. 사다
16. 상상하다　17. 등불, 램프　18. 좌석, 자리
19. 훔치다　20. 미로　21. 탈출하다; 탈출
22. 출입문, 대문　23. 순간　24. 모험

B
1. guess　2. because　3. top　4. riders　5. while
6. which　7. rapidly　8. increases　9. thrill
10. fear　11. at the same time　12. located
13. yesterday　14. thirsty　15. bought
16. imagine　17. lamp　18. seat　19. steal
20. maze　21. escape　22. gate　23. moment
24. adventure

| Review Test |

A
1. ①　2. ②　3. ③　4. ③　5. ④　6. ①　7. ②
8. ①　9. ②　10. ①　11. ④　12. ②　13. ③
14. ④　15. ②

B 16. ①　17. ③　18. ②

C 19. ②　20. ③